Templates

for the Solution of Linear Systems:
Building Blocks for Iterative Methods

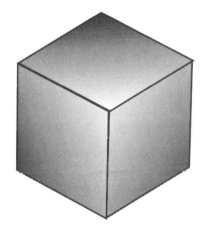

Richard Barrett
Michael Berry
Tony F. Chan
James Demmel
June Donato
Jack Dongarra
Victor Eijkhout
Roldan Pozo
Charles Romine
Henk van der Vorst

D1604662

sıam.

Society for Industrial and Applied Mathematics
Philadelphia 1994

The royalties from the sales of this book are being placed in a fund to help students attend SIAM meetings and other SIAM related activities. This fund is administered by SIAM and qualified individuals are encouraged to write directly to SIAM for guidelines. Society for Industrial and Applied Mathematics, 3600 University City Science Center, Philadelphia, Pennsylvania 19104-2688

This book is also available in Postscript form over the Internet.
To retrieve the postscript file you can use one of the following methods:

1) anonymous ftp to netlib2.cs.utk.edu
    cd linalg
    get templates.ps
    quit

2) from any machine on the Internet type:
    rcp anon@netlib2.cs.utk.edu:linalg/templates.ps templates.ps

3) sending email to netlib@ornl.gov and in the message type:
    send templates.ps from linalg

4) use Xnetlib and click "library", click "linalg", click
    "linalg/templates.ps", click "download", click "Get Files Now".
    (Xnetlib is an X-window interface to the netlib software based on a client-server model.
    The software can be found in netlib, "send index from xnetlib").

How to Use This Book

We have divided this book into five main chapters. Chapter 1 gives the motivation for this book and the use of templates.

Chapter 2 describes stationary and nonstationary iterative methods. In this chapter we present both historical development and state-of-the-art methods for solving some of the most challenging computational problems facing researchers.

Chapter 3 focuses on preconditioners. Many iterative methods depend in part on preconditioners to improve performance and ensure fast convergence.

Chapter 4 provides a glimpse of issues related to the use of iterative methods. This chapter, like the preceding, is especially recommended for the experienced user who wishes to have further guidelines for tailoring a specific code to a particular machine. It includes information on complex systems, stopping criteria, data storage formats, and parallelism.

Chapter 5 includes overviews of related topics such as the close connection between the Lanczos algorithm and the Conjugate Gradient algorithm, block iterative methods, red/black orderings, domain decomposition methods, multigrid-like methods, and row-projection schemes.

The Appendices contain information on how the templates and BLAS software can be obtained. A glossary of important terms used in the book is also provided.

The field of iterative methods for solving systems of linear equations is in constant flux, with new methods and approaches continually being created, modified, tuned, and some eventually discarded. We expect the material in this book to undergo changes from time to time as some of these new approaches mature and become the state-of-the-art. Therefore, we plan to update the material included in this book periodically for future editions. We welcome your comments and criticisms of this work to help us in that updating process. Please send your comments and questions by email to templates@cs.utk.edu.

Acknowledgements

The authors gratefully acknowledge the valuable assistance of many people who commented on preliminary drafts of this book. In particular, we thank Loyce Adams, Bill Coughran, Roland Freund, Gene Golub, Eric Grosse, Mark Jones, David Kincaid, Steve Lee, Tarek Mathew, Noël Nachtigal, Jim Ortega, and David Young for their insightful comments. We also thank Geoffrey Fox for initial discussions on the concept of templates, and Karin Remington for designing the front cover.

This work was supported in part by DARPA and ARO under contract number DAAL03-91-C-0047, the National Science Foundation Science and Technology Center Cooperative Agreement No. CCR-8809615, the Applied Mathematical Sciences subprogram of the Office of Energy Research, U.S. Department of Energy, under Contract DE-AC05-84OR21400, and the Stichting Nationale Computer Faciliteit (NCF) by Grant CRG 92.03.

Authors' Affiliations

Richard Barrett
University of Tennessee, Knoxville

Michael Berry
University of Tennessee, Knoxville

Tony F. Chan
University of California, Los Angeles

James Demmel
University of California, Berkeley

June Donato
Oak Ridge National Laboratory

Jack Dongarra
University of Tennessee, Knoxville
and Oak Ridge National Laboratory

Victor Eijkhout
University of Tennessee, Knoxville

Roldan Pozo
University of Tennessee, Knoxville

Charles Romine
Oak Ridge National Laboratory

Henk van der Vorst
Utrecht University, the Netherlands

Contents

List of Symbols

$A, \ldots, Z$	matrices
$a, \ldots, z$	vectors
$\alpha, \beta, \ldots, \omega$	scalars
A^T	matrix transpose
A^H	conjugate transpose (Hermitian) of A
A^{-1}	matrix inverse
A^{-T}	the inverse of A^T
$a_{i,j}$	matrix element
$a_{.,j}$	jth matrix column
$A_{i,j}$	matrix subblock
a_i	vector element
u_x, u_{xx}	first, second derivative with respect to x
(x,y), $x^T y$	vector dot product (inner product)
$x_j^{(i)}$	jth component of vector x in the ith iteration
diag(A)	diagonal of matrix A
diag$(\alpha, \beta \ldots)$	diagonal matrix constructed from scalars $\alpha, \beta \ldots$
span$(a, b \ldots)$	spanning space of vectors $a, b \ldots$
$\mathcal{R}$	set of real numbers
$\mathcal{R}^n$	real n-space
$\|x\|_2$	2-norm
$\|x\|_p$	p-norm
$\|x\|_A$	the "A-norm", defined as $(Ax, x)^{1/2}$
$\lambda_{\max}(A), \lambda_{\min}(A)$	eigenvalues of A with maximum (resp. minimum) modulus
$\sigma_{\max}(A), \sigma_{\min}(A)$	largest and smallest singular values of A
$\kappa_2(A)$	spectral condition number of matrix A
$\mathcal{L}$	linear operator
$\overline{\alpha}$	complex conjugate of the scalar α
max$\{S\}$	maximum value in set S
min$\{S\}$	minimum value in set S
$\sum$	summation
$O(\cdot)$	"big-oh" asymptotic bound

Conventions Used in this Book

D	diagonal matrix
L	lower triangular matrix
U	upper triangular matrix
Q	orthogonal matrix
M	preconditioner
I, $I^{n \times n}$	$n \times n$ identity matrix
$\hat{x}$	typically, the exact solution to $Ax = b$
h	discretization mesh width

List of Figures

Chapter 1

Introduction

Which of the following statements is true?

- Users want "black box" software that they can use with complete confidence for general problem classes without having to understand the fine algorithmic details.

- Users want to be able to tune data structures for a particular application, even if the software is not as reliable as that provided for general methods.

It turns out both are true, for different groups of users.

Traditionally, users have asked for and been provided with black box software in the form of mathematical libraries such as `LAPACK`, `LINPACK`, `NAG`, and `IMSL`. More recently, the high-performance community has discovered that they must write custom software for their problem. Their reasons include inadequate functionality of existing software libraries, data structures that are not natural or convenient for a particular problem, and overly general software that sacrifices too much performance when applied to a special case of interest.

Can we meet the needs of both groups of users? We believe we can. Accordingly, in this book, we introduce the use of *templates*. A template is a description of a general algorithm rather than the executable object code or the source code more commonly found in a conventional software library. Nevertheless, although templates are general descriptions of key algorithms, they offer whatever degree of customization the user may desire. For example, they can be configured for the specific data structure of a problem or for the specific computing system on which the problem is to run.

We focus on the use of iterative methods for solving large sparse systems of linear equations.

Many methods exist for solving such problems. The trick is to find the most effective method for the problem at hand. Unfortunately, a method that works well for one problem type may not work as well for another. Indeed, it may not work at all.

Thus, besides providing templates, we suggest how to choose and implement an effective method, and how to specialize a method to specific matrix types. We restrict ourselves to *iterative methods*, which work by repeatedly improving an approximate solution until it is accurate enough. These methods access the coefficient matrix A of the linear system only via the matrix-vector product $y = A \cdot x$ (and perhaps $z = A^T \cdot x$). Thus the user need only supply a subroutine for computing y (and perhaps z) given x, which permits full exploitation of the sparsity or other special structure of A.

We believe that after reading this book, applications developers will be able to use templates to get their program running on a parallel machine quickly. Nonspecialists will know how to choose and implement an approach to solve a particular problem. Specialists will be able to assemble and modify their codes—without having to make the huge investment that has, up to now, been required to tune large-scale applications for each particular machine. Finally, we hope that all users will gain a better understanding of the algorithms employed. While education has not been one of the traditional goals of mathematical software, we believe that our approach will go a long way in providing such a valuable service.

1.1 Why Use Templates?

Templates offer three significant advantages. First, templates are general and reusable. Thus, they can simplify ports to diverse machines. This feature is important given the diversity of parallel architectures.

Second, templates exploit the expertise of two distinct groups. The expert numerical analyst creates a template reflecting in-depth knowledge of a specific numerical technique. The computational scientist then provides "value-added" capability to the general template description, customizing it for specific contexts or applications needs.

And third, templates are not language specific. Rather, they are displayed in an Algol-like structure, which is readily translatable into the target language such as FORTRAN (with the use of the Basic Linear Algebra Subprograms, or BLAS, whenever possible) and C. By using these familiar styles, we believe that the users will have trust in the algorithms. We also hope that users will gain a better understanding of numerical techniques and parallel programming.

For each template, we provide some or all of the following:

- a mathematical description of the flow of the iteration;

- discussion of convergence and stopping criteria;

- suggestions for applying a method to special matrix types (*e.g.*, banded systems);

- advice for tuning (for example, which preconditioners are applicable and which are not);

- tips on parallel implementations; and

- hints as to when to use a method, and why.

For each of the templates, the following can be obtained via electronic mail.

- a MATLAB implementation based on dense matrices;

- a FORTRAN-77 program with calls to BLAS[1].

See Appendix A for details.

---

[1] For a discussion of BLAS as building blocks, see [66,67,68,141] and LAPACK routines [3]. Also, see Appendix B.

1.2 What Methods Are Covered?

Many iterative methods have been developed and it is impossible to cover them all. We chose the methods below either because they illustrate the historical development of iterative methods, or because they represent the current state-of-the-art for solving large sparse linear systems. The methods we discuss are:

1. Jacobi

2. Gauss-Seidel

3. Successive Over-Relaxation (SOR)

4. Symmetric Successive Over-Relaxation (SSOR)

5. Conjugate Gradient (CG)

6. Minimal Residual (MINRES) and Symmetric LQ (SYMMLQ)

7. Conjugate Gradients on the Normal Equations (CGNE and CGNR)

8. Generalized Minimal Residual (GMRES)

9. Biconjugate Gradient (BiCG)

10. Quasi-Minimal Residual (QMR)

11. Conjugate Gradient Squared (CGS)

12. Biconjugate Gradient Stabilized (Bi-CGSTAB)

13. Chebyshev Iteration

For each method we present a general description, including a discussion of the history of the method and numerous references to the literature. We also give the mathematical conditions for selecting a given method.

We do not intend to write a "cookbook", and have deliberately avoided the words "numerical recipes", because these phrases imply that our algorithms can be used blindly without knowledge of the system of equations. The state of the art in iterative methods does not permit this: some knowledge about the linear system is needed to guarantee convergence of these algorithms, and generally the more that is known the more the algorithm can be tuned. Thus, we have chosen to present an algorithmic outline, with guidelines for choosing a method and implementing it on particular kinds of high-performance machines. We also discuss the use of preconditioners and relevant data storage issues.

Chapter 2

Iterative Methods

The term "iterative method" refers to a wide range of techniques that use successive approximations to obtain more accurate solutions to a linear system at each step. In this book we will cover two types of iterative methods. Stationary methods are older, simpler to understand and implement, but usually not as effective. Nonstationary methods are a relatively recent development; their analysis is usually harder to understand, but they can be highly effective. The nonstationary methods we present are based on the idea of sequences of orthogonal vectors. (An exception is the Chebyshev iteration method, which is based on orthogonal polynomials.)

The rate at which an iterative method converges depends greatly on the spectrum of the coefficient matrix. Hence, iterative methods usually involve a second matrix that transforms the coefficient matrix into one with a more favorable spectrum. The transformation matrix is called a *preconditioner*. The use of a good preconditioner improves the convergence of the iterative method, sufficiently to overcome the extra cost of constructing and applying the preconditioner. Indeed, without a preconditioner the iterative method may even fail to converge.

2.1   Overview of the Methods

Below are short descriptions of each of the methods to be discussed, along with brief notes on the classification of the methods in terms of the class of matrices for which they are most appropriate. In later sections of this chapter more detailed descriptions of these methods are given.

- Stationary Methods

  - Jacobi.

    The Jacobi method is based on solving for every variable locally with respect to the other variables; one iteration of the method corresponds to solving for every variable once. The resulting method is easy to understand and implement, but convergence is slow.

  - Gauss-Seidel.

The Gauss-Seidel method is like the Jacobi method, except that it uses updated values as soon as they are available. In general, it will converge faster than the Jacobi method, though still relatively slowly.

- SOR.

  Successive Overrelaxation (SOR) can be derived from the Gauss-Seidel method by introducing an extrapolation parameter ω. For the optimal choice of ω, SOR converges faster than Gauss-Seidel by an order of magnitude.

- SSOR.

  Symmetric Successive Overrelaxation (SSOR) has no advantage over SOR as a stand-alone iterative method; however, it is useful as a preconditioner for nonstationary methods.

- Nonstationary Methods

  - Conjugate Gradient (CG).

    The conjugate gradient method derives its name from the fact that it generates a sequence of conjugate (or orthogonal) vectors. These vectors are the residuals of the iterates. They are also the gradients of a quadratic functional, the minimization of which is equivalent to solving the linear system. CG is an extremely effective method when the coefficient matrix is symmetric positive definite, since storage for only a limited number of vectors is required.

  - Minimum Residual (MINRES) and Symmetric LQ (SYMMLQ).

    These methods are computational alternatives for CG for coefficient matrices that are symmetric but possibly indefinite. SYMMLQ will generate the same solution iterates as CG if the coefficient matrix is symmetric positive definite.

  - Conjugate Gradient on the Normal Equations: CGNE and CGNR.

    These methods are based on the application of the CG method to one of two forms of the *normal equations* for $Ax = b$. CGNE solves the system $(AA^T)y = b$ for y and then computes the solution $x = A^T y$. CGNR solves $(A^T A)x = \tilde{b}$ for the solution vector x where $\tilde{b} = A^T b$. When the coefficient matrix A is nonsymmetric and nonsingular, the normal equations matrices AA^T and $A^T A$ will be symmetric and positive definite, and hence CG can be applied. The convergence may be slow, since the spectrum of the normal equations matrices will be less favorable than the spectrum of A.

  - Generalized Minimal Residual (GMRES).

    The Generalized Minimal Residual method computes a sequence of orthogonal vectors (like MINRES), and combines these through a least-squares solve and update. However, unlike MINRES (and CG) it requires storing the whole sequence, so that a large amount of storage is needed. For this reason, restarted versions of this method are used. In restarted versions, computation and storage costs are limited by specifying a fixed number of vectors to be generated. This method is useful for general nonsymmetric matrices.

- BiConjugate Gradient (BiCG).

  The Biconugate Gradient method generates two CG-like sequences of vectors, one based on a system with the original coefficient matrix A, and one on A^T. Instead of orthogonalizing each sequence, they are made mutually orthogonal, or "bi-orthogonal". This method, like CG, uses limited storage. It is useful when the matrix is nonsymmetric and nonsingular; however, convergence may be irregular, and there is a possibility that the method will break down. BiCG requires a multiplication with the coefficient matrix and with its transpose at each iteration.

- Quasi-Minimal Residual (QMR).

  The Quasi-Minimal Residual method applies a least-squares solve and update to the BiCG residuals, thereby smoothing out the irregular convergence behavior of BiCG. QMR largely avoids the breakdown that can occur in BiCG.

- Conjugate Gradient Squared (CGS).

  The Conjugate Gradient Squared method is a variant of BiCG that applies the updating operations for the A-sequence and the A^T-sequences both to the same vectors. Ideally, this would double the convergence rate, but in practice convergence may be much more irregular than for BiCG. An added practical advantage is that the method does not need the multiplications with the transpose of the coefficient matrix.

- Biconjugate Gradient Stabilized (Bi-CGSTAB).

  The Biconjugate Gradient Stabilized method is a variant of BiCG, like CGS, but using different updates for the A^T-sequence in order to obtain smoother convergence than CGS.

- Chebyshev Iteration.

  The Chebyshev Iteration recursively determines polynomials with coefficients chosen to minimize the norm of the residual in a min-max sense. The coefficient matrix must be positive definite and knowledge of the extremal eigenvalues is required. This method has the advantage of requiring no inner products.

2.2 Stationary Iterative Methods

Iterative methods that can be expressed in the simple form

$$x^{(k)} = Bx^{(k-1)} + c \tag{2.1}$$

(where neither B nor c depend upon the iteration count k) are called *stationary* iterative methods. In this section, we present the four main stationary iterative methods: the *Jacobi method*, the *Gauss-Seidel method*, the *Successive Overrelaxation (SOR) method* and the *Symmetric Successive Overrelaxation (SSOR) method*. In each case, we summarize their convergence behavior and their effectiveness, and discuss how and when they should be used. Finally, in §2.2.5, we give some historical background and further notes and references.

2.2.1   The Jacobi Method

The Jacobi method is easily derived by examining each of the n equations in the linear system $Ax = b$ in isolation. If in the ith equation

$$\sum_{j=1}^{n} a_{i,j} x_j = b_i,$$

we solve for the value of x_i while assuming the other entries of x remain fixed, we obtain

$$x_i = (b_i - \sum_{j \neq i} a_{i,j} x_j)/a_{i,i}. \tag{2.2}$$

This suggests an iterative method defined by

$$x_i^{(k)} = (b_i - \sum_{j \neq i} a_{i,j} x_j^{(k-1)})/a_{i,i}, \tag{2.3}$$

which is the Jacobi method. Note that the order in which the equations are examined is irrelevant, since the Jacobi method treats them independently. For this reason, the Jacobi method is also known as the *method of simultaneous displacements*, since the updates could in principle be done simultaneously.

In matrix terms, the definition of the Jacobi method in (2.3) can be expressed as

$$x^{(k)} = D^{-1}(L + U)x^{(k-1)} + D^{-1}b, \tag{2.4}$$

where the matrices D, $-L$ and $-U$ represent the diagonal, the strictly lower-triangular, and the strictly upper-triangular parts of A, respectively.

The pseudocode for the Jacobi method is given in Figure 2.1. Note that an auxiliary storage vector, $\bar{x}$ is used in the algorithm. It is not possible to update the vector x in place, since values from $x^{(k-1)}$ are needed throughout the computation of $x^{(k)}$.

Convergence of the Jacobi method

Iterative methods are often used for solving discretized partial differential equations. In that context a rigorous analysis of the convergence of simple methods such as the Jacobi method can be given.

As an example, consider the boundary value problem

$$\mathcal{L}u = -u_{xx} = f \qquad \text{on } (0,1), \qquad u(0) = u_0, \quad u(1) = u_1,$$

discretized by

$$Lu(x_i) = 2u(x_i) - u(x_{i-1}) - u(x_{i+1}) = f(x_i) \qquad \text{for } x_i = i/N, \, i = 1 \ldots N - 1.$$

The eigenfunctions of the $\mathcal{L}$ and L operator are the same: for $n = 1 \ldots N - 1$ the function $u_n(x) = \sin n\pi x$ is an eigenfunction corresponding to $\lambda = 2\sin^2 n\pi/(2N)$. The eigenvalues of the Jacobi iteration matrix B are then $\lambda(B) = 1 - 1/2\lambda(L) = 1 - \sin^2 n\pi/(2N)$.

From this it is easy to see that the high frequency modes (*i.e.*, eigenfunction u_n with n large) are damped quickly, whereas the damping factor for modes with n small

Choose an initial guess $x^{(0)}$ to the solution x.
for $k = 1, 2, \ldots$
    for $i = 1, 2, \ldots, n$
        $\bar{x}_i = 0$
        for $j = 1, 2, \ldots, i-1, i+1, \ldots, n$
            $\bar{x}_i = \bar{x}_i + a_{i,j} x_j^{(k-1)}$
        end
        $\bar{x}_i = (b_i - \bar{x}_i)/a_{i,i}$
    end
    $x^{(k)} = \bar{x}$
    check convergence; continue if necessary
end

Figure 2.1: The Jacobi Method

is close to 1. The spectral radius of the Jacobi iteration matrix is $\approx 1 - 5/N^2$, and it is attained for the eigenfunction $u(x) = \sin \pi x$.

The type of analysis applied to this example can be generalized to higher dimensions and other stationary iterative methods. For both the Jacobi and Gauss-Seidel method (below) the spectral radius is found to be $1 - O(h^2)$ where h is the discretization mesh width, *i.e.*, $h = N^{-d}$ where N is the number of variables and d is the number of space dimensions.

2.2.2 The Gauss-Seidel Method

Consider again the linear equations in (2.2). If we proceed as with the Jacobi method, but now assume that the equations are examined one at a time in sequence, and that previously computed results are used as soon as they are available, we obtain the Gauss-Seidel method:

$$x_i^{(k)} = (b_i - \sum_{j<i} a_{i,j} x_j^{(k)} - \sum_{j>i} a_{i,j} x_j^{(k-1)})/a_{i,i}. \tag{2.5}$$

Two important facts about the Gauss-Seidel method should be noted. First, the computations in (2.5) appear to be serial. Since each component of the new iterate depends upon all previously computed components, the updates cannot be done simultaneously as in the Jacobi method. Second, the new iterate $x^{(k)}$ depends upon the order in which the equations are examined. The Gauss-Seidel method is sometimes called the *method of successive displacements* to indicate the dependence of the iterates on the ordering. If this ordering is changed, the *components* of the new iterate (and not just their order) will also change.

These two points are important because if A is sparse, the dependency of each component of the new iterate on previous components is not absolute. The presence of zeros in the matrix may remove the influence of some of the previous components. Using a judicious ordering of the equations, it may be possible to reduce such dependence,

Choose an initial guess $x^{(0)}$ to the solution x.
for $k = 1, 2, \ldots$
    for $i = 1, 2, \ldots, n$
        $\sigma = 0$
        for $j = 1, 2, \ldots, i - 1$
            $\sigma = \sigma + a_{i,j} x_j^{(k)}$
        end
        for $j = i + 1, \ldots, n$
            $\sigma = \sigma + a_{i,j} x_j^{(k-1)}$
        end
        $x_i^{(k)} = (b_i - \sigma)/a_{i,i}$
    end
    check convergence; continue if necessary
end

Figure 2.2: The Gauss-Seidel Method

thus restoring the ability to make updates to groups of components in parallel. How-ever, reordering the equations can affect the rate at which the Gauss-Seidel method converges. A poor choice of ordering can degrade the rate of convergence; a good choice can enhance the rate of convergence. For a practical discussion of this trade-off (parallelism versus convergence rate) and some standard reorderings, the reader is referred to Chapter 3 and §4.4.

In matrix terms, the definition of the Gauss-Seidel method in (2.5) can be expressed as

$$x^{(k)} = (D - L)^{-1}(U x^{(k-1)} + b). \tag{2.6}$$

As before, D, $-L$ and $-U$ represent the diagonal, lower-triangular, and upper-triangular parts of A, respectively.

The pseudocode for the Gauss-Seidel algorithm is given in Figure 2.2.

2.2.3   The Successive Overrelaxation Method

The Successive Overrelaxation Method, or SOR, is devised by applying extrapolation to the Gauss-Seidel method. This extrapolation takes the form of a weighted average between the previous iterate and the computed Gauss-Seidel iterate successively for each component:

$$x_i^{(k)} = \omega \bar{x}_i^{(k)} + (1 - \omega) x_i^{(k-1)}$$

(where $\bar{x}$ denotes a Gauss-Seidel iterate, and ω is the extrapolation factor). The idea is to choose a value for ω that will accelerate the rate of convergence of the iterates to the solution.

In matrix terms, the SOR algorithm can be written as follows:

Choose an initial guess $x^{(0)}$ to the solution x.
for $k = 1, 2, \ldots$
    for $i = 1, 2, \ldots, n$
        $\sigma = 0$
        for $j = 1, 2, \ldots, i - 1$
            $\sigma = \sigma + a_{i,j} x_j^{(k)}$
        end
        for $j = i + 1, \ldots, n$
            $\sigma = \sigma + a_{i,j} x_j^{(k-1)}$
        end
        $\sigma = (b_i - \sigma)/a_{i,i}$
        $x_i^{(k)} = x_i^{(k-1)} + \omega(\sigma - x_i^{(k-1)})$
    end
    check convergence; continue if necessary
end

Figure 2.3: The SOR Method

$$x^{(k)} = (D - \omega L)^{-1}(\omega U + (1 - \omega)D)x^{(k-1)} + \omega(D - \omega L)^{-1}b. \qquad (2.7)$$

The pseudocode for the SOR algorithm is given in Figure 2.3.

Choosing the Value of ω

If $\omega = 1$, the SOR method simplifies trivially back to the Gauss-Seidel method. A theorem due to Kahan [130] shows that SOR fails to converge if ω is outside the interval $(0, 2)$. Though technically the term *underrelaxation* should be used when $0 < \omega < 1$, for convenience the term overrelaxation is now used for any value of $\omega \in (0, 2)$.

In general, it is not possible to compute in advance the value of ω that is optimal with respect to the rate of convergence of SOR. Even when it is possible to compute the optimal value for ω, the expense of such computation is usually prohibitive. Frequently, some heuristic estimate is used, such as $\omega = 2 - O(h)$ where h is the mesh spacing of the discretization of the underlying physical domain.

If the coefficient matrix A is symmetric and positive definite, the SOR iteration is guaranteed to converge for *any* value of ω between 0 and 2, though the choice of ω can significantly affect the rate at which the SOR iteration converges. Sophisticated implementations of the SOR algorithm (such as that found in ITPACK [138]) employ adaptive parameter estimation schemes to try to home in on the appropriate value of ω by estimating the rate at which the iteration is converging.

For coefficient matrices of a special class called *consistently ordered with property A* (see Young [212]), which includes certain orderings of matrices arising from the discretization of elliptic PDEs, there is a direct relationship between the spectra of the Jacobi and SOR iteration matrices. In principle, given the spectral radius ρ of the Jacobi iteration matrix, one can determine *a priori* the theoretically optimal value of ω for SOR:

$$\omega_{\text{opt}} = \frac{2}{1 + \sqrt{1 - \rho^2}}. \tag{2.8}$$

This is seldom done, since calculating the spectral radius of the Jacobi matrix requires an impractical amount of computation. However, relatively inexpensive rough estimates of ρ (for example, from the power method, see Golub and Van Loan [108, p. 351]) can yield reasonable estimates for the optimal value of ω.

2.2.4   The Symmetric Successive Overrelaxation Method

If we assume that the coefficient matrix A is symmetric, then the Symmetric Successive Overrelaxation method, or SSOR, combines two SOR sweeps together in such a way that the resulting iteration matrix is similar to a symmetric matrix. Specifically, the first SOR sweep is carried out as in (2.7), but in the second sweep the unknowns are updated in the reverse order. That is, SSOR is a forward SOR sweep followed by a backward SOR sweep. The similarity of the SSOR iteration matrix to a symmetric matrix permits the application of SSOR as a preconditioner for other iterative schemes for symmetric matrices. Indeed, this is the primary motivation for SSOR since its convergence rate, with an optimal value of ω, is usually *slower* than the convergence rate of SOR with optimal ω (see Young [212, page 462]). For details on using SSOR as a preconditioner, see Chapter 3.

   In matrix terms, the SSOR iteration can be expressed as follows:

$$x^{(k)} = B_1 B_2 x^{(k-1)} + \omega(2 - \omega)(D - \omega U)^{-1}D(D - \omega L)^{-1}b, \tag{2.9}$$

where

$$B_1 = (D - \omega U)^{-1}(\omega L + (1 - \omega)D),$$

and

$$B_2 = (D - \omega L)^{-1}(\omega U + (1 - \omega)D).$$

Note that B_2 is simply the iteration matrix for SOR from (2.7), and that B_1 is the same, but with the roles of L and U reversed.

   The pseudocode for the SSOR algorithm is given in Figure 2.4.

2.2.5   Notes and References

The modern treatment of iterative methods dates back to the relaxation method of Southwell [189]. This was the precursor to the SOR method, though the order in which approximations to the unknowns were relaxed varied during the computation. Specifically, the next unknown was chosen based upon estimates of the location of the largest error in the current approximation. Because of this, Southwell's relaxation method was considered impractical for automated computing. It is interesting to note that the introduction of multiple-instruction, multiple data-stream (MIMD) parallel computers has rekindled an interest in so-called *asynchronous*, or *chaotic* iterative methods (see Chazan and Miranker [52], Baudet [29], and Elkin [88]), which are closely related to Southwell's original relaxation method. In chaotic methods, the order of relaxation

Choose an initial guess $x^{(0)}$ to the solution x.
for $k = 1, 2, \ldots$
    for $i = 1, 2, \ldots, n$
        $\sigma = 0$
        for $j = 1, 2, \ldots, i - 1$
            $\sigma = \sigma + a_{i,j} x_j^{(k-\frac{1}{2})}$
        end
        for $j = i + 1, \ldots, n$
            $\sigma = \sigma + a_{i,j} x_j^{(k-1)}$
        end
        $\sigma = (b_i - \sigma)/a_{i,i}$
        $x_i^{(k-\frac{1}{2})} = x_i^{(k-1)} + \omega(\sigma - x_i^{(k-1)})$
    end
    for $i = n, n - 1, \ldots, 1$
        $\sigma = 0$
        for $j = 1, 2, \ldots, i - 1$
            $\sigma = \sigma + a_{i,j} x_j^{(k-\frac{1}{2})}$
        end
        for $j = i + 1, \ldots, n$
            $\sigma = \sigma + a_{i,j} x_j^{(k)}$
        end
        $x_i^{(k)} = x_i^{(k-\frac{1}{2})} + \omega(\sigma - x_i^{(k-\frac{1}{2})})$
    end
    check convergence; continue if necessary
end

Figure 2.4: The SSOR Method

is unconstrained, thereby eliminating costly synchronization of the processors, though the effect on convergence is difficult to predict.

The notion of accelerating the convergence of an iterative method by extrapolation predates the development of SOR. Indeed, Southwell used overrelaxation to accelerate the convergence of his original relaxation method. More recently, the *ad hoc SOR* method, in which a different relaxation factor ω is used for updating each variable, has given impressive results for some classes of problems (see Ehrlich [80]).

The three main references for the theory of stationary iterative methods are Varga [206], Young [212] and Hageman and Young [119]. The reader is referred to these books (and the references therein) for further details concerning the methods described in this section.

2.3 Nonstationary Iterative Methods

Nonstationary methods differ from stationary methods in that the computations involve information that changes at each iteration. Typically, constants are computed by taking inner products of residuals, or other vectors arising from the iterative method.

2.3.1 Conjugate Gradient Method (CG)

The Conjugate Gradient method is an effective method for symmetric positive definite systems. It is the oldest and best known of the nonstationary methods discussed here. The method proceeds by generating vector sequences of iterates (*i.e.*, successsive approximations to the solution), residuals corresponding to the iterates, and search directions used in updating the iterates and residuals. Although the length of these sequences can become large, only a small number of vectors needs to be kept in memory. In every iteration of the method, two inner products are performed in order to compute update scalars that are defined to make the sequences satisfy certain orthogonality conditions. On a symmetric positive definite linear system these conditions imply that the distance to the true solution is minimized in some norm.

The iterates $x^{(i)}$ are updated in each iteration by a multiple (α_i) of the search direction vector $p^{(i)}$:

$$x^{(i)} = x^{(i-1)} + \alpha_i p^{(i)}.$$

Correspondingly the residuals $r^{(i)} = b - Ax^{(i)}$ are updated as

$$r^{(i)} = r^{(i-1)} - \alpha q^{(i)} \qquad \text{where} \qquad q^{(i)} = Ap^{(i)}. \tag{2.10}$$

The choice $\alpha = \alpha_i = r^{(i)T} r^{(i)}/p^{(i)T} Ap^{(i)}$ minimizes $r^{(i)T} A^{-1} r^{(i)}$ over all possible choices for α in equation (2.10).

The search directions are updated using the residuals

$$p^{(i)} = r^{(i)} + \beta_{i-1} p^{(i-1)}, \tag{2.11}$$

where the choice $\beta_i = r^{(i)T} r^{(i)}/r^{(i-1)T} r^{(i-1)}$ ensures that $p^{(i)}$ and $Ap^{(i-1)}$ – or equivalently, $r^{(i)}$ and $r^{(i-1)}$ – are orthogonal. In fact, one can show that this choice of β_i makes $p^{(i)}$ and $r^{(i)}$ orthogonal to *all* previous $Ap^{(j)}$ and $r^{(j)}$ respectively.

The pseudocode for the Preconditioned Conjugate Gradient Method is given in Figure 2.5. It uses a preconditioner M; for $M = I$ one obtains the unpreconditioned version of the Conjugate Gradient Algorithm. In that case the algorithm may be further simplified by skipping the "solve" line, and replacing $z^{(i-1)}$ by $r^{(i-1)}$ (and $z^{(0)}$ by $r^{(0)}$).

Theory

The unpreconditioned conjugate gradient method constructs the ith iterate $x^{(i)}$ as an element of $x^{(0)} + \text{span}\{r^{(0)}, \ldots, A^{i-1} r^{(0)}\}$ so that $(x^{(i)} - \hat{x})^T A(x^{(i)} - \hat{x})$ is minimized, where $\hat{x}$ is the exact solution of $Ax = b$. This minimum is guaranteed to exist in general only if A is symmetric positive definite. The preconditioned version of the method uses a different subspace for constructing the iterates, but it satisfies the same minimization property, although over this different subspace. It requires in addition that the preconditioner M is symmetric and positive definite.

Compute $r^{(0)} = b - Ax^{(0)}$ for some initial guess $x^{(0)}$
for $i = 1, 2, \ldots$
    solve $Mz^{(i-1)} = r^{(i-1)}$
    $\rho_{i-1} = r^{(i-1)^T} z^{(i-1)}$
    if $i = 1$
        $p^{(1)} = z^{(0)}$
    else
        $\beta_{i-1} = \rho_{i-1}/\rho_{i-2}$
        $p^{(i)} = z^{(i-1)} + \beta_{i-1}p^{(i-1)}$
    endif
    $q^{(i)} = Ap^{(i)}$
    $\alpha_i = \rho_{i-1}/p^{(i)^T} q^{(i)}$
    $x^{(i)} = x^{(i-1)} + \alpha_i p^{(i)}$
    $r^{(i)} = r^{(i-1)} - \alpha_i q^{(i)}$
    check convergence; continue if necessary
end

Figure 2.5: The Preconditioned Conjugate Gradient Method

The above minimization of the error is equivalent to the residuals $r^{(i)} = b - Ax^{(i)}$ being M^{-1} orthogonal (that is, $r^{(i)^T} M^{-1} r^{(j)} = 0$ if $i \neq j$). Since for symmetric A an orthogonal basis for the Krylov subspace span$\{r^{(0)}, \ldots, A^{i-1}r^{(0)}\}$ can be constructed with only three-term recurrences, such a recurrence also suffices for generating the residuals. In the Conjugate Gradient method two coupled two-term recurrences are used; one that updates residuals using a search direction vector, and one updating the search direction with a newly computed residual. This makes the Conjugate Gradient Method quite attractive computationally.

There is a close relationship between the Conjugate Gradient method and the Lanczos method for determining eigensystems, since both are based on the construction of an orthogonal basis for the Krylov subspace. In fact, the coefficients computed during the CG iteration can be used to reconstruct the Lanczos process, and the other way around; see Paige and Saunders [164] and Golub and Van Loan [108, §10.2.6]. This relationship can be exploited to obtain relevant information about the eigensystem of the (preconditioned) matrix A; see §5.1.

Convergence

Accurate predictions of the convergence of iterative methods are difficult to make, but useful bounds can often be obtained. For the Conjugate Gradient method, the error can be bounded in terms of the spectral condition number κ_2 of the matrix $M^{-1}A$. (Recall that if $\lambda_{\max}$ and $\lambda_{\min}$ are the largest and smallest eigenvalues of a symmetric positive definite matrix B, then the spectral condition number of B is $\kappa_2(B) = \lambda_{\max}(B)/\lambda_{\min}(B)$). If $\hat{x}$ is the exact solution of the linear system $Ax = b$, with symmetric positive definite matrix A, then for CG with symmetric positive definite preconditioner M, it can be shown that

$$\|x^{(i)} - \hat{x}\|_A \leq 2\alpha^i \|x^{(0)} - \hat{x}\|_A \tag{2.12}$$

where $\alpha = (\sqrt{\kappa_2} - 1)/(\sqrt{\kappa_2} + 1)$ (see Golub and Van Loan [108, §10.2.8], and Kaniel [131]), and $\|y\|_A^2 \equiv (y, Ay)$. From this relation we see that the number of iterations to reach a relative reduction of ϵ in the error is proportional to $\sqrt{\kappa_2}$.

In some cases, practical application of the above error bound is straightforward. For example, elliptic second order partial differential equations typically give rise to coefficient matrices A with $\kappa_2(A) = O(h^{-2})$ (where h is the discretization mesh width), independent of the order of the finite elements or differences used, and of the number of space dimensions of the problem (see for instance Axelsson and Barker [14, §5.5]). Thus, without preconditioning, we expect a number of iterations proportional to h^{-1} for the Conjugate Gradient method.

Other results concerning the behavior of the Conjugate Gradient algorithm have been obtained. If the extremal eigenvalues of the matrix $M^{-1}A$ are well separated, then one often observes so-called *superlinear convergence* (see Concus, Golub and O'Leary [56]); that is, convergence at a rate that increases per iteration. This phenomenon is explained by the fact that CG tends to eliminate components of the error in the direction of eigenvectors associated with extremal eigenvalues first. After these have been eliminated, the method proceeds as if these eigenvalues did not exist in the given system, *i.e.*, the convergence rate depends on a reduced system with a (much) smaller condition number (for an analysis of this, see Van der Sluis and Van der Vorst [194]). The effectiveness of the preconditioner in reducing the condition number and in separating extremal eigenvalues can be deduced by studying the approximated eigenvalues of the related Lanczos process.

Implementation

The Conjugate Gradient method involves one matrix-vector product, three vector updates, and two inner products per iteration. Some slight computational variants exist that have the same structure (see Reid [174]). Variants that cluster the inner products, a favorable property on parallel machines, are discussed in §4.4.

For a discussion of the Conjugate Gradient method on vector and shared memory computers, see Dongarra, *et al.* [68,162]. For discussions of the method for more general parallel architectures see Demmel, Heath and Van der Vorst [64] and Ortega [162], and the references therein.

Further references

A more formal presentation of CG, as well as many theoretical properties, can be found in the textbook by Hackbusch [117]. Shorter presentations are given in Axelsson and Barker [14] and Golub and Van Loan [108]. An overview of papers published in the first 25 years of existence of the method is given in Golub and O'Leary [107].

2.3.2   MINRES and SYMMLQ

The Conjugate Gradient method can be viewed as a special variant of the Lanczos method (see §5.1) for positive definite symmetric systems. The MINRES and SYMMLQ methods are variants that can be applied to symmetric indefinite systems.

The vector sequences in the Conjugate Gradient method correspond to a factorization of a tridiagonal matrix similar to the coefficient matrix. Therefore, a breakdown of the algorithm can occur corresponding to a zero pivot if the matrix is indefinite. Furthermore, for indefinite matrices the minimization property of the Conjugate Gradient method is no longer well-defined. The MINRES and SYMMLQ methods are variants of the CG method that avoid the LU-factorization and do not suffer from breakdown. MINRES minimizes the residual in the 2-norm. SYMMLQ solves the projected system, but does not minimize anything (it keeps the residual orthogonal to all previous ones). The convergence behavior of Conjugate Gradients and MINRES for indefinite systems was analyzed by Paige, Parlett, and Van der Vorst [163].

Theory

When A is not positive definite, but symmetric, we can still construct an orthogonal basis for the Krylov subspace by three term recurrence relations. Eliminating the search directions in equations (2.10) and (2.11) gives a recurrence

$$Ar^{(i)} = r^{(i+1)}t_{i+1,i} + r^{(i)}t_{i,i} + r^{(i-1)}t_{i-1,i},$$

which can be written in matrix form as

$$AR_i = R_{i+1}\bar{T}_i,$$

where $\bar{T}_i$ is an $(i+1) \times i$ tridiagonal matrix

$$\bar{T}_i = \begin{pmatrix} \ddots & & \ddots & & \\ \ddots & \ddots & & \ddots & \\ & \ddots & \ddots & & \ddots \\ & & \ddots & \ddots & \\ & & & \ddots & \end{pmatrix} \quad \begin{matrix} \uparrow \\ i+1 \\ \downarrow \end{matrix}$$

In this case we have the problem that $(\cdot, \cdot)_A$ no longer defines an inner product. However we can still try to minimize the residual in the 2-norm by obtaining

$$x^{(i)} \in \{r^{(0)}, Ar^{(0)}, \ldots, A^{i-1}r^{(0)}\}, \quad x^{(i)} = R_i\bar{y}$$

that minimizes

$$\|Ax^{(i)} - b\|_2 = \|AR_i\bar{y} - b\|_2 = \|R_{i+1}\bar{T}_iy - b\|_2.$$

Now we exploit the fact that if $D_{i+1} \equiv \text{diag}(\|r^{(0)}\|_2, \|r^{(1)}\|_2, \ldots, \|r^{(i)}\|_2)$, then $R_{i+1}D_{i+1}^{-1}$ is an orthonormal transformation with respect to the current Krylov subspace:

$$\|Ax^{(i)} - b\|_2 = \|D_{i+1}\bar{T}_iy - \|r^{(0)}\|_2e^{(1)}\|_2$$

and this final expression can simply be seen as a minimum norm least squares problem.

The element in the $(i+1, i)$ position of $\bar{T}_i$ can be annihilated by a simple Givens rotation and the resulting upper bidiagonal system (the other subdiagonal elements having been removed in previous iteration steps) can simply be solved, which leads to the MINRES method (see Paige and Saunders [164]).

Another possibility is to solve the system $T_i y = \|r^{(0)}\|_2 e^{(1)}$, as in the CG method ($T_i$ is the upper $i \times i$ part of $\bar{T}_i$). Other than in CG we cannot rely on the existence of a Choleski decomposition (since A is not positive definite). An alternative is then to decompose T_i by an LQ-decomposition. This again leads to simple recurrences and the resulting method is known as SYMMLQ (see Paige and Saunders [164]).

2.3.3 CG on the Normal Equations, CGNE and CGNR

The CGNE and CGNR methods are the simplest methods for nonsymmetric or indefinite systems. Since other methods for such systems are in general rather more complicated than the Conjugate Gradient method, transforming the system to a symmetric definite one and then applying the Conjugate Gradient method is attractive for its coding simplicity.

Theory

If a system of linear equations $Ax = b$ has a nonsymmetric, possibly indefinite (but nonsingular), coefficient matrix, one obvious attempt at a solution is to apply Conjugate Gradient to a related *symmetric positive definite* system, $A^T A x = A^T b$. While this approach is easy to understand and code, the convergence speed of the Conjugate Gradient method now depends on the square of the condition number of the original coefficient matrix. Thus the rate of convergence of the CG procedure on the normal equations may be slow.

Several proposals have been made to improve the numerical stability of this method. The best known is by Paige and Saunders [165] and is based upon applying the Lanczos method to the auxiliary system

$$\begin{pmatrix} I & A \\ A^T & 0 \end{pmatrix} \begin{pmatrix} r \\ x \end{pmatrix} = \begin{pmatrix} b \\ 0 \end{pmatrix}.$$

A clever execution of this scheme delivers the factors L and U of the LU-decomposition of the tridiagonal matrix that would have been computed by carrying out the Lanczos procedure with $A^T A$.

Another means for improving the numerical stability of this normal equations approach is suggested by Björck and Elfving in [33]. The observation that the matrix $A^T A$ is used in the construction of the iteration coefficients through an inner product like $(p, A^T A p)$ leads to the suggestion that such an inner product be replaced by (Ap, Ap).

2.3.4 Generalized Minimal Residual (GMRES)

The Generalized Minimal Residual method is an extension of MINRES (which is only applicable to symmetric systems) to unsymmetric systems. Like MINRES, it generates a sequence of orthogonal vectors, but in the absence of symmetry this can no longer be done with short recurrences; instead, all previously computed vectors in the orthogonal sequence have to be retained. For this reason, "restarted" versions of the method are used.

In the Conjugate Gradient method, the residuals form an orthogonal basis for the space span$\{r^{(0)}, Ar^{(0)}, A^2r^{(0)}, \ldots\}$. In GMRES, this basis is formed explicitly:

$w^{(i)} = Av^{(i)}$
for $k = 1, \ldots, i$
$\qquad w^{(i)} = w^{(i)} - (w^{(i)}, v^{(k)})v^{(k)}$
end
$v^{(i+1)} = w^{(i)}/\|w^{(i)}\|$

The reader may recognize this as a modified Gram-Schmidt orthogonalization. Applied to the Krylov sequence $\{A^k r^{(0)}\}$ this orthogonalization is called the "Arnoldi method" [6]. The inner product coefficients $(w^{(i)}, v^{(k)})$ and $\|w^{(i)}\|$ are stored in a Hessenberg matrix.

The GMRES iterates are constructed as

$$x^{(i)} = x^{(0)} + y_1 v^{(1)} + \cdots + y_i v^{(i)},$$

where the coefficients y_k have been chosen to minimize the residual norm $\|b - Ax^{(i)}\|$. The GMRES algorithm has the property that this residual norm can be computed without the iterate having been formed. Thus, the expensive action of forming the iterate can be postponed until the residual norm is deemed small enough.

The pseudocode for the restarted GMRES(m) algorithm with preconditioner M is given in Figure 2.6.

Theory

The Generalized Minimum Residual (GMRES) method is designed to solve nonsymmetric linear systems (see Saad and Schultz [185]). The most popular form of GMRES is based on the modified Gram-Schmidt procedure, and uses restarts to control storage requirements.

If no restarts are used, GMRES (like any orthogonalizing Krylov-subspace method) will converge in no more than n steps (assuming exact arithmetic). Of course this is of no practical value when n is large; moreover, the storage and computational requirements in the absence of restarts are prohibitive. Indeed, the crucial element for successful application of GMRES(m) revolves around the decision of when to restart; that is, the choice of m. Unfortunately, there exist examples for which the method stagnates and convergence takes place only at the nth step. For such systems, any choice of m less than n fails to converge.

Saad and Schultz [185] have proven several useful results. In particular, they show that if the coefficient matrix A is real and *nearly* positive definite, then a "reasonable" value for m may be selected. Implications of the choice of m are discussed below.

Implementation

A common implementation of GMRES is suggested by Saad and Schultz in [185] and relies on using modified Gram-Schmidt orthogonalization. Householder transformations, which are relatively costly but stable, have also been proposed. The Householder approach results in a three-fold increase in work; however, convergence may be better, especially for ill-conditioned systems (see Walker [209]). From the point of view of

$x^{(0)}$ is an initial guess
for $j = 1, 2, ...$
    Solve r from $Mr = b - Ax^{(0)}$
    $v^{(1)} = r/\|r\|_2$
    $s := \|r\|_2 e_1$
    for $i = 1, 2, ..., m$
        Solve w from $Mw = Av^{(i)}$
        for $k = 1, ..., i$
            $h_{k,i} = (w, v^{(k)})$
            $w = w - h_{k,i} v^{(k)}$
        end
        $h_{i+1,i} = \|w\|_2$
        $v^{(i+1)} = w/h_{i+1,i}$
        apply $J_1, ..., J_{i-1}$ on $(h_{1,i}, ..., h_{i+1,i})$
        construct J_i, acting on ith and $(i + 1)$st component
        of $h_{.,i}$, such that $(i + 1)$st component of $J_i h_{.,i}$ is 0
        $s := J_i s$
        if $s(i + 1)$ is small enough then (UPDATE($\tilde{x}, i$) and quit)
    end
    UPDATE($\tilde{x}, m$)
end

In this scheme UPDATE($\tilde{x}, i$)
replaces the following computations:

Compute y as the solution of $Hy = \tilde{s}$, in which
the upper $i \times i$ triangular part of H has $h_{i,j}$ as
its elements (in least squares sense if H is singular),
$\tilde{s}$ represents the first i components of s
$\tilde{x} = x^{(0)} + y^{(1)} v^{(1)} + y^{(2)} v^{(2)} + ... + y^{(i)} v^{(i)}$
$s^{(i+1)} = \|b - A\tilde{x}\|_2$
if $\tilde{x}$ is an accurate enough approximation then quit
else $x^{(0)} = \tilde{x}$

Figure 2.6: The Preconditioned GMRES(m) Method

parallelism, Gram-Schmidt orthogonalization may be preferred, giving up some stability for better parallelization properties (see Demmel, Heath and Van der Vorst [64]). Here we adopt the Modified Gram-Schmidt approach.

The major drawback to GMRES is that the amount of work and storage required per iteration rises linearly with the iteration count. Unless one is fortunate enough to obtain extremely fast convergence, the cost will rapidly become prohibitive. The usual way to overcome this limitation is by restarting the iteration. After a chosen number (m) of iterations, the accumulated data are cleared and the intermediate results are used as the initial data for the next m iterations. This procedure is repeated until convergence is achieved. The difficulty is in choosing an appropriate value for m. If m is "too small", GMRES(m) may be slow to converge, or fail to converge entirely. A value of m that is larger than necessary involves excessive work (and uses more storage). Unfortunately, there are no definite rules governing the choice of m—choosing when to restart is a matter of experience.

For a discussion of GMRES for vector and shared memory computers see Dongarra et al. [68]; for more general architectures, see Demmel, Heath and Van der Vorst [64].

2.3.5   BiConjugate Gradient (BiCG)

The Conjugate Gradient method is not suitable for nonsymmetric systems because the residual vectors cannot be made orthogonal with short recurrences (for proof of this see Voevodin [208] or Faber and Manteuffel [92]). The GMRES method retains orthogonality of the residuals by using long recurrences, at the cost of a larger storage demand. The BiConjugate Gradient method takes another approach, replacing the orthogonal sequence of residuals by two mutually orthogonal sequences, at the price of no longer providing a minimization.

The update relations for residuals in the Conjugate Gradient method are augmented in the BiConjugate Gradient method by similar relations, but based on A^T instead of A. Thus we update two sequences of residuals

$$r^{(i)} = r^{(i-1)} - \alpha_i A p^{(i)}, \qquad \tilde{r}^{(i)} = \tilde{r}^{(i-1)} - \alpha_i A^T \tilde{p}^{(i)},$$

and two sequences of search directions

$$p^{(i)} = r^{(i-1)} + \beta_{i-1} p^{(i-1)}, \qquad \tilde{p}^{(i)} = \tilde{r}^{(i-1)} + \beta_{i-1} \tilde{p}^{(i-1)}.$$

The choices

$$\alpha_i = \frac{\tilde{r}^{(i-1)^T} r^{(i-1)}}{\tilde{p}^{(i)^T} A p^{(i)}}, \qquad \beta_i = \frac{\tilde{r}^{(i)^T} r^{(i)}}{\tilde{r}^{(i-1)^T} r^{(i-1)}}$$

ensure the bi-orthogonality relations

$$\tilde{r}^{(i)^T} r^{(j)} = \tilde{p}^{(i)^T} A p^{(j)} = 0 \qquad \text{if } i \neq j.$$

The pseudocode for the Preconditioned BiConjugate Gradient Method with preconditioner M is given in Figure 2.7.

Compute $r^{(0)} = b - Ax^{(0)}$ for some initial guess $x^{(0)}$.
Choose $\tilde{r}^{(0)}$ (for example, $\tilde{r}^{(0)} = r^{(0)}$).
for $i = 1, 2, \ldots$
    solve $Mz^{(i-1)} = r^{(i-1)}$
    solve $M^T \tilde{z}^{(i-1)} = \tilde{r}^{(i-1)}$
    $\rho_{i-1} = z^{(i-1)^T} \tilde{r}^{(i-1)}$
    if $\rho_{i-1} = 0$, **method fails**
    if $i = 1$
        $p^{(i)} = z^{(i-1)}$
        $\tilde{p}^{(i)} = \tilde{z}^{(i-1)}$
    else
        $\beta_{i-1} = \rho_{i-1}/\rho_{i-2}$
        $p^{(i)} = z^{(i-1)} + \beta_{i-1} p^{(i-1)}$
        $\tilde{p}^{(i)} = \tilde{z}^{(i-1)} + \beta_{i-1} \tilde{p}^{(i-1)}$
    endif
    $q^{(i)} = Ap^{(i)}$
    $\tilde{q}^{(i)} = A^T \tilde{p}^{(i)}$
    $\alpha_i = \rho_{i-1}/\tilde{p}^{(i)^T} q^{(i)}$
    $x^{(i)} = x^{(i-1)} + \alpha_i p^{(i)}$
    $r^{(i)} = r^{(i-1)} - \alpha_i q^{(i)}$
    $\tilde{r}^{(i)} = \tilde{r}^{(i-1)} - \alpha_i \tilde{q}^{(i)}$
    check convergence; continue if necessary
end

Figure 2.7: The Preconditioned BiConjugate Gradient Method

Convergence

Few theoretical results are known about the convergence of BiCG. For symmetric positive definite systems the method delivers the same results as CG, but at twice the cost per iteration. For nonsymmetric matrices it has been shown that in phases of the process where there is significant reduction of the norm of the residual, the method is more or less comparable to full GMRES (in terms of numbers of iterations) (see Freund and Nachtigal [100]). In practice this is often confirmed, but it is also observed that the convergence behavior may be quite irregular, and the method may even break down. The breakdown situation due to the possible event that $z^{(i-1)^T} \tilde{r}^{(i-1)} \approx 0$ can be circumvented by so-called look-ahead strategies (see Parlett, Taylor and Liu [168]). This leads to complicated codes and is beyond the scope of this book. The other breakdown situation, $\tilde{p}^{(i)^T} q^{(i)} \approx 0$, occurs when the LU-decomposition fails (see §2.3.5), and can be repaired by using another decomposition. This is done in QMR (see §2.3.6).

Sometimes, breakdown or near-breakdown situations can be satisfactorily avoided by a restart at the iteration step immediately before the (near-) breakdown step.

Another possibility is to switch to a more robust (but possibly more expensive) method, like GMRES.

Implementation

BiCG requires computing a matrix-vector product $Ap^{(k)}$ and a transpose product $A^T \tilde{p}^{(k)}$. In some applications the latter product may be impossible to perform, for instance if the matrix is not formed and the regular product is only given as an operation.

In a parallel environment, the two matrix-vector products can theoretically be performed simultaneously; however, in a distributed-memory environment, there will be extra communication costs associated with one of the two matrix-vector products, depending upon the storage scheme for A. A duplicate copy of the matrix will alleviate this problem, at the cost of doubling the storage requirements for the matrix.

Care must also be exercised in choosing the preconditioner, since similar problems arise during the two solves involving the preconditioning matrix.

It is difficult to make a fair comparison between GMRES and BiCG. GMRES really minimizes a residual, but at the cost of increasing work for keeping all residuals orthogonal and increasing demands for memory space. BiCG does not minimize a residual, but often its accuracy is comparable to GMRES, at the cost of twice the amount of matrix vector products per iteration step. However, the generation of the basis vectors is relatively cheap and the memory requirements are modest. Several variants of BiCG have been proposed that increase the effectiveness of this class of methods in certain circumstances. These variants (CGS and Bi-CGSTAB) will be discussed in coming subsections.

2.3.6   Quasi-Minimal Residual (QMR)

The BiConjugate Gradient method often displays rather irregular convergence behavior. Moreover, the implicit LU decomposition of the reduced tridiagonal system may not exist, resulting in breakdown of the algorithm. A related algorithm, the Quasi-Minimal Residual method of Freund and Nachtigal [100], [101] attempts to overcome these problems. The main idea behind this algorithm is to solve the reduced tridiagonal system in a least squares sense, similar to the approach followed in GMRES. Since the constructed basis for the Krylov subspace is bi-orthogonal, rather than orthogonal as in GMRES, the obtained solution is viewed as a quasi-minimal residual solution, which explains the name. Additionally, QMR uses look-ahead techniques to avoid breakdowns in the underlying Lanczos process, which makes it more robust than BiCG.

Convergence

The convergence behavior of QMR is typically much smoother than for BiCG. Freund and Nachtigal [100] present quite general error bounds which show that QMR may be expected to converge about as fast as GMRES. From a relation between the residuals in BiCG and QMR (Freund and Nachtigal [100, relation (5.10)]) one may deduce that at phases in the iteration process where BiCG makes significant progress, QMR has

Compute $r^{(0)} = b - Ax^{(0)}$ for some initial guess $x^{(0)}$
$\tilde{v}^{(1)} = r^{(0)}$; solve $M_1 y = \tilde{v}^{(1)}$; $\rho_1 = \|y\|_2$
Choose $\tilde{w}^{(1)}$, for example $\tilde{w}^{(1)} = r^{(0)}$
solve $M_2 z = \tilde{w}^{(1)}$; $\xi_1 = \|z\|_2$
$\gamma_0 = 1; \eta_0 = -1$
for $i = 1, 2, \ldots$
 if $\rho_i = 0$ or $\xi_i = 0$ method fails
 $v^{(i)} = \tilde{v}^{(i)}/\rho_i$; $y = y/\rho_i$
 $w^{(i)} = \tilde{w}^{(i)}/\xi_i$; $z = z/\xi_i$
 $\delta_i = z^T y$; if $\delta_i = 0$ method fails
 solve $M_2 \tilde{y} = y$
 solve $M_1^T \tilde{z} = z$
 if $i = 1$
  $p^{(1)} = \tilde{y}$; $q^{(1)} = \tilde{z}$
  else
  $p^{(i)} = \tilde{y} - (\xi_i \delta_i / \epsilon_{i-1}) p^{(i-1)}$
  $q^{(i)} = \tilde{z} - (\rho_i \delta_i / \epsilon_{i-1}) q^{(i-1)}$
 endif
 $\tilde{p} = A p^{(i)}$
 $\epsilon_i = {q^{(i)}}^T \tilde{p}$; if $\epsilon_i = 0$ method fails
 $\beta_i = \epsilon_i / \delta_i$; if $\beta_i = 0$ method fails
 $\tilde{v}^{(i+1)} = \tilde{p} - \beta_i v^{(i)}$
 solve $M_1 y = \tilde{v}^{(i+1)}$
 $\rho_{i+1} = \|y\|_2$
 $\tilde{w}^{(i+1)} = A^T q^{(i)} - \beta_i w^{(i)}$
 solve $M_2^T z = \tilde{w}^{(i+1)}$
 $\xi_{i+1} = \|z\|_2$
 $\theta_i = \rho_{i+1}/(\gamma_{i-1}|\beta_i|)$; $\gamma_i = 1/\sqrt{1 + \theta_i^2}$; if $\gamma_i = 0$ method fails
 $\eta_i = -\eta_{i-1} \rho_i \gamma_i^2 / (\beta_i \gamma_{i-1}^2)$
 if $i = 1$
  $d^{(1)} = \eta_1 p^{(1)}$; $s^{(1)} = \eta_1 \tilde{p}$
  else
  $d^{(i)} = \eta_i p^{(i)} + (\theta_{i-1} \gamma_i)^2 d^{(i-1)}$
  $s^{(i)} = \eta_i \tilde{p} + (\theta_{i-1} \gamma_i)^2 s^{(i-1)}$
 endif
 $x^{(i)} = x^{(i-1)} + d^{(i)}$
 $r^{(i)} = r^{(i-1)} - s^{(i)}$
 check convergence; continue if necessary
end

Figure 2.8: The Preconditioned Quasi Minimal Residual Method without Look-ahead

arrived at about the same approximation for $\hat{x}$. On the other hand, when BiCG makes no progress at all, QMR may still show slow convergence.

The look-ahead steps in the QMR method prevent breakdown in all cases but the so-called "incurable breakdown".

Implementation

The pseudocode for the Preconditioned Quasi Minimal Residual Method, with preconditioner $M = M_1 M_2$, is given in Figure 2.8. This algorithm follows the two term recurrence version without look-ahead, presented by Freund and Nachtigal [101] as Algorithm 7.1. This version of QMR is simpler to implement than the full QMR method with look-ahead, but it is susceptible to breakdown of the underlying Lanczos process. (Other implementational variations are whether to scale Lanczos vectors or not, or to use three-term recurrences instead of coupled two-term recurrences. Such decisions usually have implications for the stability and the efficiency of the algorithm.) A professional implementation of QMR with look-ahead is given in Freund and Nachtigal's QMRPACK, which is available through netlib; see Appendix A.

We have modified the algorithm to include a relatively inexpensive recurrence relation for the computation of the residual vector. This requires a few extra vectors of storage and vector update operations per iteration, but it avoids expending a matrix-vector product on the residual calculation. Also, the algorithm has been modified so that only two full preconditioning steps are required instead of three.

Computation of the residual is done for the convergence test. If one uses right (or post) preconditioning, that is $M_1 = I$, then a cheap upper bound for $\|r^{(i)}\|$ can be computed in each iteration, avoiding the recursions for $r^{(i)}$. For details, see Freund and Nachtigal [100, proposition 4.1]. This upper bound may be pessimistic by a factor of at most $\sqrt{i+1}$.

QMR has roughly the same problems with respect to vector and parallel implementation as BiCG. The scalar overhead per iteration is slightly more than for BiCG. In all cases where the slightly cheaper BiCG method converges irregularly (but fast enough), there seems little reason to avoid QMR.

2.3.7 Conjugate Gradient Squared Method (CGS)

In BiCG, the residual vector $r^{(i)}$ can be regarded as the product of $r^{(0)}$ and an ith degree polynomial in A, that is

$$r^{(i)} = P_i(A)r^{(0)}.$$ (2.13)

This same polynomial satisfies $\tilde{r}^{(i)} = P_i(A)\tilde{r}^{(0)}$ so that

$$\rho_i = (\tilde{r}^{(i)}, r^{(i)}) = (P_i(A^T)\tilde{r}^{(0)}, P_i(A)r^{(0)}) = (\tilde{r}^{(i)}, P_i^2(A)r^{(0)}).$$ (2.14)

This suggests that if $P_i(A)$ reduces $r^{(0)}$ to a smaller vector $r^{(i)}$, then it might be advantageous to apply this "contraction" operator twice, and compute $P_i^2(A)r^{(0)}$. Equation (2.14) shows that the iteration coefficients can still be recovered from these vectors, and it turns out to be easy to find the corresponding approximations for x. This approach leads to the Conjugate Gradient Squared method (see Sonneveld [188]).

Compute $r^{(0)} = b - Ax^{(0)}$ for some initial guess $x^{(0)}$
Choose $\tilde{r}$ (for example, $\tilde{r} = r^{(0)}$)
for $i = 1, 2, \ldots$
$\quad \rho_{i-1} = \tilde{r}^T r^{(i-1)}$
$\quad$ **if** $\rho_{i-1} = 0$ **method fails**
$\quad$ **if** $i = 1$
$\quad\quad u^{(1)} = r^{(0)}$
$\quad\quad p^{(1)} = u^{(1)}$
$\quad$ **else**
$\quad\quad \beta_{i-1} = \rho_{i-1}/\rho_{i-2}$
$\quad\quad u^{(i)} = r^{(i-1)} + \beta_{i-1} q^{(i-1)}$
$\quad\quad p^{(i)} = u^{(i)} + \beta_{i-1}(q^{(i-1)} + \beta_{i-1} p^{(i-1)})$
$\quad$ **endif**
$\quad$ **solve** $M\hat{p} = p^{(i)}$
$\quad \hat{v} = A\hat{p}$
$\quad \alpha_i = \rho_{i-1}/\tilde{r}^T \hat{v}$
$\quad q^{(i)} = u^{(i)} - \alpha_i \hat{v}$
$\quad$ **solve** $M\hat{u} = u^{(i)} + q^{(i)}$
$\quad x^{(i)} = x^{(i-1)} + \alpha_i \hat{u}$
$\quad \hat{q} = A\hat{u}$
$\quad r^{(i)} = r^{(i-1)} - \alpha_i \hat{q}$
$\quad$ check convergence; continue if necessary
end

Figure 2.9: The Preconditioned Conjugate Gradient Squared Method

Convergence

Often one observes a speed of convergence for CGS that is about twice as fast as for BiCG, which is in agreement with the observation that the same "contraction" operator is applied twice. However, there is no reason that the "contraction" operator, even if it really reduces the initial residual $r^{(0)}$, should also reduce the once reduced vector $r^{(k)} = P_k(A)r^{(0)}$. This is evidenced by the often highly irregular convergence behavior of CGS. One should be aware of the fact that local corrections to the current solution may be so large that cancellation effects occur. This may lead to a less accurate solution than suggested by the updated residual (see Van der Vorst [202]). The method tends to diverge if the starting guess is close to the solution.

Implementation

CGS requires about the same number of operations per iteration as BiCG, but does not involve computations with A^T. Hence, in circumstances where computation with A^T is impractical, CGS may be attractive.

The pseudocode for the Preconditioned Conjugate Gradient Squared Method with

---

Compute $r^{(0)} = b - Ax^{(0)}$ for some initial guess $x^{(0)}$
Choose $\tilde{r}$ (for example, $\tilde{r} = r^{(0)}$)
for $i = 1, 2, \ldots$
    $\rho_{i-1} = \tilde{r}^T r^{(i-1)}$
    if $\rho_{i-1} = 0$ **method fails**
    if $i = 1$
        $p^{(i)} = r^{(i-1)}$
    else
        $\beta_{i-1} = (\rho_{i-1}/\rho_{i-2})(\alpha_{i-1}/\omega_{i-1})$
        $p^{(i)} = r^{(i-1)} + \beta_{i-1}(p^{(i-1)} - \omega_{i-1}v^{(i-1)})$
    endif
    solve $M\hat{p} = p^{(i)}$
    $v^{(i)} = A\hat{p}$
    $\alpha_i = \rho_{i-1}/\tilde{r}^T v^{(i)}$
    $s = r^{(i-1)} - \alpha_i v^{(i)}$
    check norm of s; if small enough: set $x^{(i)} = x^{(i-1)} + \alpha_i\hat{p}$ and stop
    solve $M\hat{s} = s$
    $t = A\hat{s}$
    $\omega_i = t^T s/t^T t$
    $x^{(i)} = x^{(i-1)} + \alpha_i\hat{p}^{(i)} + \omega_i\hat{s}$
    $r^{(i)} = s - \omega_i t$
    check convergence; continue if necessary
    for continuation it is necessary that $\omega_i \neq 0$
end

Figure 2.10: The Preconditioned BiConjugate Gradient Stabilized Method

preconditioner M is given in Figure 2.9.

2.3.8 BiConjugate Gradient Stabilized (Bi-CGSTAB)

The BiConjugate Gradient Stabilized method (Bi-CGSTAB) was developed to solve nonsymmetric linear systems while avoiding the often irregular convergence patterns of the Conjugate Gradient Squared method (see Van der Vorst [202]). Instead of computing the CGS sequence $i \mapsto P_i^2(A)r^{(0)}$, Bi-CGSTAB computes $i \mapsto Q_i(A)P_i(A)r^{(0)}$ where Q_i is an ith degree polynomial describing a steepest descent update.

Convergence

Bi-CGSTAB often converges about as fast as CGS, sometimes faster and sometimes not. CGS can be viewed as a method in which the BiCG "contraction" operator is applied twice. Bi-CGSTAB can be interpreted as the product of BiCG and repeatedly applied GMRES(1). At least locally, a residual vector is minimized, which leads to a considerably smoother convergence behavior. On the other hand, if the local GMRES(1) step stagnates, then the Krylov subspace is not expanded, and Bi-CGSTAB will break down. This is a breakdown situation that can occur in addition to the other breakdown possiblities in the underlying BiCG algorithm. This type of breakdown may be avoided by combining BiCG with other methods, *i.e.*, by selecting other values for ω_i (see the algorithm). One such alternative is Bi-CGSTAB2 (see Gutknecht [114]); more general approaches are suggested by Sleijpen and Fokkema in [186].

Implementation

Bi-CGSTAB requires two matrix-vector products and four inner products, *i.e.*, two inner products more than BiCG and CGS.

   The pseudocode for the Preconditioned BiConjugate Gradient Stabilized Method with preconditioner M is given in Figure 2.10.

2.3.9   Chebyshev Iteration

Chebyshev Iteration is another method for solving nonsymmetric problems (see Golub and Van Loan [108, §10.1.5] and Varga [206, Chapter 5]). Chebyshev Iteration avoids the computation of inner products as is necessary for the other nonstationary methods. For some distributed memory architectures these inner products are a bottleneck with respect to efficiency. The price one pays for avoiding inner products is that the method requires enough knowledge about the spectrum of the coefficient matrix A that an ellipse enveloping the spectrum can be identified; however this difficulty can be overcome via an adaptive construction developed by Manteuffel [143], and implemented by Ashby [7]. Chebyshev iteration is suitable for any nonsymmetric linear system for which the enveloping ellipse does not include the origin.

Comparison with other methods

Comparing the pseudocode for Chebyshev Iteration with the pseudocode for the Conjugate Gradient method shows a high degree of similarity, except that no inner products are computed in Chebyshev Iteration.

   Scalars c and d must be selected so that they define a family of ellipses with common center $d > 0$ and foci $d + c$ and $d - c$ which contain the ellipse that encloses the spectrum of A and for which the rate r of convergence is minimal:

$$r = \frac{a + \sqrt{a^2 - c^2}}{d + \sqrt{d^2 - c^2}}, \tag{2.15}$$

where a is the length of the x-axis of the ellipse.

   We provide code in which it is assumed that c and d are known. For code including the adaptive detemination of these iteration parameters the reader is referred to Ashby [7]. The Chebyshev method has the advantage over GMRES that only short recurrences are used. On the other hand, GMRES is guaranteed to generate the smallest residual over the current search space. The BiCG methods, which also use short recurrences, do not minimize the residual in a suitable norm; however, unlike Chebyshev iteration, they do not require estimation of parameters (the spectrum of A).

Finally, GMRES and BiCG may be more effective in practice, because of superlinear convergence behavior, which cannot be expected for Chebyshev.

For symmetric positive definite systems the "ellipse" enveloping the spectrum degenerates to the interval $[\lambda_{\min}, \lambda_{\max}]$ on the positive x-axis, where $\lambda_{\min}$ and $\lambda_{\max}$ are the smallest and largest eigenvalues of $M^{-1}A$. In circumstances where the computation of inner products is a bottleneck, it may be advantageous to start with CG, compute estimates of the extremal eigenvalues from the CG coefficients, and then after sufficient convergence of these approximations switch to Chebyshev Iteration. A similar strategy may be adopted for a switch from GMRES, or BiCG-type methods, to Chebyshev Iteration.

Convergence

In the symmetric case (where A and the preconditioner M are both symmetric) for the Chebyshev Iteration we have the same upper bound as for the Conjugate Gradient method, provided c and d are computed from λ_{min} and λ_{max} (the extremal eigenvalues of the preconditioned matrix $M^{-1}A$).

There is a severe penalty for overestimating or underestimating the field of values. For example, if in the symmetric case λ_{max} is underestimated, then the method may diverge; if it is overestimated then the result may be very slow convergence. Similar statements can be made for the nonsymmetric case. This implies that one needs fairly accurate bounds on the spectrum of $M^{-1}A$ for the method to be effective (in comparison with CG or GMRES).

Implementation

In Chebyshev Iteration the iteration parameters are known as soon as one knows the ellipse containing the eigenvalues (or rather, the field of values) of the operator. Therefore the computation of inner products, as is necessary in methods like GMRES or CG, is avoided. This avoids the synchronization points required of CG-type methods, so machines with hierarchical or distributed memory may achieve higher performance (it also suggests strong parallelization properties; for a discussion of this see Saad [181], and Dongarra, *et al.* [68]). Specifically, as soon as some segment of w is computed, we may begin computing, in sequence, corresponding segments of p, x, and r.

The pseudocode for the Preconditioned Chebyshev Method with preconditioner M is given in Figure 2.11. It handles the case of a symmetric positive definite coefficient matrix A. The eigenvalues of $M^{-1}A$ are assumed to be all real and in the interval $[\lambda_{min}, \lambda_{max}]$, which does not include zero.

2.4 Summary of the Methods

Implementing an effective iterative method for solving a linear system cannot be done without some knowledge of the linear system. If good performance is important, consideration must also be given to the computational kernels of the method and how efficiently they can be executed on the target architecture. This point is of particular importance on parallel architectures; see §4.4.

In this section we summarize for each method

Compute $r^{(0)} = b - Ax^{(0)}$ for some initial guess $x^{(0)}$.
$d = (\lambda_{\max} + \lambda_{\min})/2$, $c = (\lambda_{\max} - \lambda_{\min})/2$.
for $i = 1, 2, \ldots$
    solve $Mz^{(i-1)} = r^{(i)}$.
    if $i = 1$
        $p^{(1)} = z^{(0)}$
        $\alpha_1 = 2/d$
    else
        $\beta_{i-1} = (c\alpha_{i-1}/2)^2$
        $\alpha_i = 1/(d - \beta_{i-1})$
        $p^{(i)} = z^{(i-1)} + \beta_{i-1}p^{(i-1)}$.
    endif
    $x^{(i)} = x^{(i-1)} + \alpha_i p^{(i)}$.
    $r^{(i)} = b - Ax^{(i)}$ $(= r^{(i-1)} - \alpha_i Ap^{(i)})$.
    check convergence; continue if necessary
end

Figure 2.11: The Preconditioned Chebyshev Method

- Matrix properties. Not every method will work on every problem type, so knowledge of matrix properties is the main criterion for selecting an iterative method.

- Computational kernels. Methods differ in the operations that they perform. However, the fact that one method uses more operations than another is not necessarily a reason for rejecting it.

  Moreover, it should be noted that for iterative methods applied to sparse systems of equations typically a lower performance is to be expected than for direct solution methods for dense systems. The sparsity of the matrix impedes reuse of data in the processor cache, and the indirect addressing of compressed storage schemes inhibits efficient pipelining of operations. Dongarra and Van der Vorst [71] give some experimental results about this, and provide a benchmark code for iterative solvers.

Table 2.2 lists the storage required for each method (without preconditioning). Note that we are not including the original system $Ax = b$ and we ignore scalar storage.

1. Jacobi Method

   - Extremely easy to use, but unless the matrix is "strongly" diagonally dominant, this method is probably best only considered as an introduction to iterative methods or as a preconditioner in a nonstationary method.

   - Trivial to parallelize.

2. Gauss-Seidel Method

Method	Inner Product	SAXPY	Matrix-Vector Product	Precond Solve
JACOBI			1^a	
GS		1	1^a	
SOR		1	1^a	
CG	2	3	1	1
GMRES	$i+1$	$i+1$	1	1
BiCG	2	5	1/1	1/1
QMR	2	$8+4^{bc}$	1/1	1/1
CGS	2	6	2	2
Bi-CGSTAB	4	6	2	2
CHEBYSHEV		2	1	1

Table 2.1: Summary of Operations for Iteration i. "a/b" means "a" multiplications with the matrix and "b" with its transpose.

---

[a] This method performs no real matrix vector product or preconditioner solve, but the number of operations is equivalent to a matrix-vector multiply.
[b] True SAXPY operations + vector scalings.
[c] Less for implementations that do not recursively update the residual.

Method	Storage Reqmts
JACOBI	matrix $+ 3n$
SOR	matrix $+ 2n$
CG	matrix $+ 6n$
GMRES	matrix $+ (i+5)n$
BiCG	matrix $+ 10n$
CGS	matrix $+ 11n$
Bi-CGSTAB	matrix $+ 10n$
QMR	matrix $+ 16n^c$
CHEBYSHEV	matrix $+ 5n$

Table 2.2: Storage Requirements for the Methods in iteration i: n denotes the order of the matrix.

---

[c] Less for implementations that do not recursively update the residual.

- Typically faster convergence than Jacobi, but in general not competitive with the nonstationary methods.
- Applicable to strictly diagonally dominant, or symmetric positive definite matrices.
- Parallelization properties depend on structure of the coefficient matrix. Different orderings of the unknowns have different degrees of parallelism; multi-color orderings give almost full parallelism.
- This is a special case of the SOR method, obtained by choosing $\omega = 1$.

3. Successive Over-Relaxation (SOR)

- Accelerates convergence of Gauss-Seidel ($\omega > 1$, *over*-relaxation); may yield convergence when Gauss-Seidel fails ($0 < \omega < 1$, *under*-relaxation).

- Speed of convergence depends critically on ω; the optimal value for ω may be estimated from the spectral radius of the Jacobi iteration matrix under certain conditions.

- Parallelization properties are the same as those of the Gauss-Seidel method.

4. Conjugate Gradient (CG)

- Applicable to symmetric positive definite systems.

- Speed of convergence depends on the condition number; if extremal eigenvalues are well-separated then superlinear convergence behavior can result.

- Inner products act as synchronization points in a parallel environment.

- Further parallel properties are largely independent of the coefficient matrix, but depend strongly on the structure the preconditioner.

5. Generalized Minimal Residual (GMRES)

- Applicable to nonsymmetric matrices.

- GMRES leads to the smallest residual for a fixed number of iteration steps, but these steps become increasingly expensive.

- In order to limit the increasing storage requirments and work per iteration step, restarting is necessary. When to do so depends on A and the right-hand side; it requires skill and experience.

- GMRES requires only matrix-vector products with the coefficient matrix.

- The number of inner products grows linearly with the iteration number, up to the restart point. In an implementation based on a simple Gram-Schmidt process the inner products are independent, so together they imply only one synchronization point. A more stable implementation based on modified Gram-Schmidt orthogonalization has one synchronization point per inner product.

6. Biconjugate Gradient (BiCG)

- Applicable to nonsymmetric matrices.

- Requires matrix-vector products with the coefficient matrix and its transpose. This disqualifies the method for cases where the matrix is only implicitly given as an operator, and the transpose therefore not available at all.

- Parallelization properties are similar to those for CG; the two matrix vector products (as well as the preconditioning steps) are independent, so they can be done in parallel, or their communication stages can be packaged.

7. Quasi-Minimal Residual (QMR)

- Applicable to nonsymmetric matrices.

- Designed to avoid the irregular convergence behavior of BiCG, it avoids one of the two breakdown situations of BiCG.

- If BiCG makes significant progress in one iteration step, then QMR delivers about the same result at the same step. But when BiCG temporarily stagnates or diverges, QMR may still further reduce the residual, albeit very slowly.

- Computational costs per iteration are similar to BiCG, but slightly higher. The method requires the transpose matrix-vector product.

- Parallelization properties are as for BiCG.

8. Conjugate Gradient Squared (CGS)

   - Applicable to nonsymmetric matrices.

   - Converges (diverges) typically about twice as fast as BiCG.

   - Convergence behavior is often quite irregular, which may lead to a loss of accuracy in the updated residual. Tends to diverge if the starting guess is close to the solution.

   - Computational costs per iteration are similar to BiCG, but the method doesn't require the transpose matrix.

   - Unlike BiCG, the two matrix-vector products are not independent, so the number of synchronization points in a parallel environment is larger.

9. Biconjugate Gradient Stabilized (Bi-CGSTAB)

   - Applicable to nonsymmetric matrices.

   - Computational costs per iteration are similar to BiCG and CGS, but the method doesn't require the transpose matrix.

   - An alternative for CGS that avoids the irregular convergence patterns of CGS while maintaining about the same speed of convergence; as a result we observe often less loss of accuracy in the updated residual.

10. Chebyshev Iteration

    - Applicable to nonsymmetric matrices (but presented in this book only for the symmetric case).

    - This method requires some explicit knowledge of the spectrum (or field of values); in the symmetric case the iteration parameters are easily obtained from the two extremal eigenvalues, which can be estimated either directly from the matrix, or from applying a few iterations of the Conjugate Gradient Method.

    - The computational structure is similar to that of CG, but there are no synchronization points.

    - The Adaptive Chebyshev method can be used in combination with methods as CG or GMRES, to continue the iteration once suitable bounds on the spectrum have been obtained from these methods.

Selecting the "best" method for a given class of problems is largely a matter of trial and error. It also depends on how much storage one has available (GMRES), on the availability of A^T (BiCG and QMR), and on how expensive the matrix vector products (and Solve steps with M) are in comparison to SAXPYs and inner products. If these matrix vector products are relatively expensive, and if sufficient storage is available then it may be attractive to use GMRES and delay restarting as much as possible.

Table 2.1 shows the type of operations performed per iteration. Based on the particular problem or data structure, the user may observe that a particular operation could be performed more efficiently.

2.5   A short history of Krylov methods[1]

Methods based on orthogonalization were developed by a number of authors in the early '50s. Lanczos' method [139] was based on two mutually orthogonal vector sequences, and his motivation came from eigenvalue problems. In that context, the most prominent feature of the method is that it reduces the original matrix to tridiagonal form. Lanczos later applied his method to solving linear systems, in particular symmetric ones [140]. An important property for proving convergence of the method when solving linear systems is that the iterates are related to the initial residual by multiplication with a polynomial in the coefficient matrix.

The joint paper by Hestenes and Stiefel [121], after their independent discovery of the same method, is the classical description of the conjugate gradient method for solving linear systems. Although error-reduction properties are proved, and experiments showing premature convergence are reported, the conjugate gradient method is presented here as a direct method, rather than an iterative method.

This Hestenes/Stiefel method is closely related to a reduction of the Lanczos method to symmetric matrices, reducing the two mutually orthogonal sequences to one orthogonal sequence, but there is an important algorithmic difference. Whereas Lanczos used three-term recurrences, the method by Hestenes and Stiefel uses coupled two-term recurrences. By combining the two two-term recurrences (eliminating the "search directions") the Lanczos method is obtained.

A paper by Arnoldi [6] further discusses the Lanczos biorthogonalization method, but it also presents a new method, combining features of the Lanczos and Hestenes/Stiefel methods. Like the Lanczos method it is applied to nonsymmetric systems, and it does not use search directions. Like the Hestenes/Stiefel method, it generates only one, self-orthogonal sequence. This last fact, combined with the asymmetry of the coefficient matrix means that the method no longer effects a reduction to tridiagonal form, but instead one to upper Hessenberg form. Presented as "minimized iterations in the Galerkin method" this algorithm has become known as the *Arnoldi algorithm*.

The conjugate gradient method received little attention as a practical method for some time, partly because of a misperceived importance of the finite termination property. Reid [174] pointed out that the most important application area lay in sparse definite systems, and this renewed the interest in the method.

---

[1]For a more detailed account of the early history of CG methods, we refer the reader to Golub and O'Leary [107] and Hestenes [122].

Several methods have been developed in later years that employ, most often implicitly, the upper Hessenberg matrix of the Arnoldi method. For an overview and characterization of these orthogonal projection methods for nonsymmetric systems see Ashby, Manteuffel and Saylor [10], Saad and Schultz [184], and Jea and Young [124].

Fletcher [94] proposed an implementation of the Lanczos method, similar to the Conjugate Gradient method, with two coupled two-term recurrences, which he named the *bi-conjugate gradient method* (BiCG).

2.6 Survey of recent Krylov methods

Research into the design of Krylov subspace methods for solving nonsymmetric linear systems is an active field of research and new methods are still emerging. In this book, we have included only the best known and most popular methods, and in particular those for which extensive computational experience has been gathered. In this section, we shall briefly highlight some of the recent developments and other methods not treated here. A survey of methods up to about 1991 can be found in Freund, Golub and Nachtigal [98]. Two more recent reports by Meier-Yang [148] and Tong [192] have extensive numerical comparisons among various methods, including several more recent ones that have not been discussed in detail in this book.

Several suggestions have been made to reduce the increase in memory and computational costs in GMRES. An obvious one is to restart (this one is included in §2.3.4): GMRES(m). Another approach is to restrict the GMRES search to a suitable subspace of some higher-dimensional Krylov subspace. Methods based on this idea can be viewed as preconditioned GMRES methods. The simplest ones exploit a fixed polynomial preconditioner (see Johnson, Micchelli and Paul [125], Saad [178], and Nachtigal, Reichel and Trefethen [155]). In more sophisticated approaches, the polynomial preconditioner is adapted to the iterations (Saad [183]), or the preconditioner may even be some other (iterative) method of choice (Van der Vorst and Vuik [204], Axelsson and Vassilevski [23]). Stagnation is prevented in the GMRESR method (Van der Vorst and Vuik [204]) by including LSQR steps in some phases of the process. In Desturler and Fokkema [61], part of the optimality of GMRES is maintained in the hybrid method GCRO, in which the iterations of the preconditioning method are kept orthogonal to the iterations of the underlying GCR method. All these approaches have advantages for some problems, but it is far from clear *a priori* which strategy is preferable in any given case.

Recent work has focused on endowing the BiCG method with several desirable properties: (1) avoiding breakdown; (2) avoiding use of the transpose; (3) efficient use of matrix-vector products; (4) smooth convergence; and (5) exploiting the work expended in forming the Krylov space with A^T for further reduction of the residual.

As discussed before, the BiCG method can have two kinds of breakdown: *Lanczos breakdown* (the underlying Lanczos process breaks down), and *pivot breakdown* (the tridiagonal matrix T implicitly generated in the underlying Lanczos process encounters a zero pivot when Gaussian elimination without pivoting is used to factor it). Although such exact breakdowns are very rare in practice, near breakdowns can cause severe numerical stability problems.

The pivot breakdown is the easier one to overcome and there have been several approaches proposed in the literature. It should be noted that for symmetric matrices,

Lanczos breakdown cannot occur and the only possible breakdown is pivot breakdown. The SYMMLQ and QMR methods discussed in this book circumvent pivot breakdown by solving least squares systems. Other methods tackling this problem can be found in Fletcher [95], Saad [176], Gutknecht [113], and Bank and Chan [25,28].

Lanczos breakdown is much more difficult to eliminate. Recently, considerable attention has been given to analyzing the nature of the Lanczos breakdown (see Parlett [168], and Gutknecht [112,115]), as well as various look-ahead techniques for remedying it (see Brezinski and Sadok [38], Brezinski, Zaglia and Sadok [39,40], Freund and Nachtigal [100], Parlett [168], Nachtigal [156], Freund, Gutknecht and Nachtigal [105], Joubert [129], Freund, Golub and Nachtigal [104], and Gutknecht [112,115]). However, the resulting algorithms are usually too complicated to give in template form (some codes of Freund and Nachtigal are available on `netlib`.) Moreover, it is still not possible to eliminate breakdowns that require look-ahead steps of arbitrary size (incurable breakdowns). So far, these methods have not yet received much practical use but some form of look-ahead may prove to be a crucial component in future methods.

In the BiCG method, the need for matrix-vector multiplies with A^T can be inconvenient as well as doubling the number of matrix-vector multiplies compared with CG for each increase in the degree of the underlying Krylov subspace. Several recent methods have been proposed to overcome this drawback. The most notable of these is the ingenious CGS method by Sonneveld [188] discussed earlier, which computes the square of the BiCG polynomial without requiring A^T – thus obviating the need for A^T. When BiCG converges, CGS is often an attractive, faster converging alternative. However, CGS also inherits (and often magnifies) the breakdown conditions and the irregular convergence of BiCG (see Van der Vorst [202]).

CGS also generated interest in the possibility of *product* methods, which generate iterates corresponding to a product of the BiCG polynomial with another polynomial of the same degree, chosen to have certain desirable properties but computable without recourse to A^T. The Bi-CGSTAB method of Van der Vorst [202] is such an example, in which the auxiliary polynomial is defined by a local minimization chosen to smooth the convergence behavior. Gutknecht [114] noted that Bi-CGSTAB could be viewed as a product of BiCG and GMRES(1), and he suggested combining BiCG with GMRES(2) for the even numbered iteration steps. This was anticipated to lead to better convergence for the case where the eigenvalues of A are complex. A more efficient and more robust variant of this approach has been suggested by Sleijpen and Fokkema in [186], where they describe how to easily combine BiCG with any GMRES(m), for modest m.

Many other basic methods can also be squared. For example, by squaring the Lanczos procedure, Chan, de Pillis and Van der Vorst [44] obtained transpose-free implementations of BiCG and QMR. By squaring the QMR method, Freund and Szeto [102] derived a transpose-free QMR squared method which is quite competitive with CGS but with much smoother convergence. Unfortunately, these methods require an extra matrix-vector product per step (three instead of two) which makes them less efficient.

In addition to Bi-CGSTAB, several recent product methods have been designed to smooth the convergence of CGS. One idea is to use the quasi-minimal residual (QMR) principle to obtain smoothed iterates from the Krylov subspace generated by other product methods. Freund [103] proposed such a QMR version of CGS, which he called TFQMR. Numerical experiments show that TFQMR in most cases retains the desirable convergence features of CGS while correcting its erratic behavior. The transpose free nature of TFQMR, its low computational cost and its smooth convergence behavior make it an attractive alternative to CGS. On the other hand, since the BiCG polynomial is still used, TFQMR breaks down whenever CGS does. One possible remedy would be to combine TFQMR with a look-ahead Lanczos technique but this appears to be quite complicated and no methods of this kind have yet appeared in the literature. Recently, Chan *et. al.* [45] derived a similar QMR version of Van der Vorst's Bi-CGSTAB method, which is called QMRCGSTAB. These methods offer smoother convergence over CGS and Bi-CGSTAB with little additional cost.

There is no clear best Krylov subspace method at this time, and there will never be a best *overall* Krylov subspace method. Each of the methods is a winner in a specific problem class, and the main problem is to identify these classes and to construct new methods for uncovered classes. The paper by Nachtigal, Reddy and Trefethen [154] shows that for any of a group of methods (CG, BiCG, GMRES, CGNE, and CGS), there is a class of problems for which a given method is the winner and another one is the loser. This shows clearly that there will be no ultimate method. The best we can hope for is some expert system that guides the user in his/her choice. Hence, iterative methods will never reach the robustness of direct methods, nor will they beat direct methods for all problems. For some problems iterative schemes and for others direct methods (or multigrid) will be most attractive. We hope to find suitable methods (and preconditioners) for classes of very large problems that we are yet unable to solve by any known method, because of CPU-restrictions, memory, convergence problems, ill-conditioning, et cetera.

Chapter 3

Preconditioners

3.1 The why and how

As we have seen, the convergence rate of iterative methods depends on spectral properties of the coefficient matrix. Hence one may attempt to transform the linear system into one that is equivalent in the sense that it has the same solution, but that has more favorable spectral properties. A *preconditioner* is a matrix that effects such a transformation.

For instance, if a matrix M approximates the coefficient matrix A in some way, the transformed system

$$M^{-1}Ax = M^{-1}b$$

has the same solution as the original system $Ax = b$, but the spectral properties of its coefficient matrix $M^{-1}A$ may be more favorable.

In devising a preconditioner, we are faced with a choice between finding a matrix M that approximates A, and for which solving a system is easier than solving one with A, or finding a matrix M that approximates A^{-1}, so that only multiplication by M is needed. The majority of preconditioners falls in the first category; a notable example of the second category will be discussed in §3.5.

3.1.1 Cost trade-off

Since applying a preconditioner incurs some extra cost, both initially and per iteration, there is a trade-off between the cost of constructing and applying the preconditioner, and the gain in convergence speed. Certain preconditioners need no construction phase at all (for instance the SSOR preconditioner), but for others, such as incomplete factorizations, there can be substantial work involved. Although the work in scalar terms may be comparable to a single iteration, the construction of the preconditioner may not be vectorizable/parallelizable even if application of the preconditioner is. In that case, the initial cost has to be amortized over the iterations, or over repeated use of the same preconditioner in multiple linear systems.

Most preconditioners take in their application an amount of work proportional to the number of variables. This implies that they multiply the work per iteration by a constant factor. On the other hand, the number of iterations as a function of the matrix size is usually only improved by a constant. Certain preconditioners are able to improve on this situation, most notably the modified incomplete factorizations and preconditioners based on multigrid techniques.

On parallel machines there is a further trade-off between the efficacy of a preconditioner in the classical sense, and its parallel efficiency. Many of the traditional preconditioners have a large sequential component.

3.1.2   Theoretical prerequisites on preconditioners

The above transformation of the linear system $A \rightarrow M^{-1}A$ is not what is used in practice. A more correct way of introducing the preconditioner would be to split the preconditioner as $M = M_1 M_2$ and to transform the system as

$$M_1^{-1}AM_2^{-1}(M_2 x) = M_1^{-1}b.$$

The matrices M_1 and M_2 are called the *left-* and *right preconditioners*, respectively.

An iterative method can be preconditioned according to the following scheme:

1. Transform the right hand side vector $b \leftarrow M_1^{-1}b$.

2. Apply the (unpreconditioned) iterative method, replacing the coefficient matrix A by $M_1^{-1}AM_2^{-1}$; call the resulting solution y.

3. Compute $x = M_2^{-1}y$.

The important theoretical point is that the transformed coefficient matrix $M_1^{-1}AM_2^{-1}$ preserves some theoretical properties of A and M: if A is symmetric and positive definite and $M_1 = M_2^T$, then the transformed coefficient matrix is again symmetric and positive definite.

Since symmetry and definiteness are crucial to the success of some iterative methods, this transformation is to be preferred over $M^{-1}A$, which is not guaranteed to be either symmetric or definite, even if A and M are.

It is a remarkable property of many iterative methods that the splitting of M is in practice not needed. By rewriting the steps of the method (see for instance Axelsson and Barker [14, pgs. 16,29] or Golub and Van Loan [108, §10.3]) it is usually possible to reintroduce a computational step

> solve u from $Mu = v$,

that is, a step that applies the preconditioner in its entirety.

3.2   Jacobi Preconditioning

The simplest preconditioner consists of just the diagonal of the matrix:

$$m_{i,j} = \begin{cases} a_{i,i} & \text{if } i = j \\ 0 & \text{otherwise.} \end{cases}$$

This is known as the (point) Jacobi preconditioner.

It is possible to use this preconditioner without using any extra storage beyond that of the matrix itself. However, division operations are usually quite costly, so in practice storage is allocated for the reciprocals of the matrix diagonal. This strategy applies to many preconditioners below.

3.2.1   Block Jacobi Methods

Block versions of the Jacobi preconditioner can be derived by a partitioning of the variables. If the index set $S = \{1, \ldots, n\}$ is partitioned as $S = \bigcup_i S_i$ with the sets S_i mutually disjoint, then

$$m_{i,j} = \begin{cases} a_{i,j} & \text{if } i \text{ and } j \text{ are in the same index subset} \\ 0 & \text{otherwise.} \end{cases}$$

The preconditioner is now a block-diagonal matrix.

Often, natural choices for the partitioning suggest themselves:

- In problems with multiple physical variables per node, blocks can be formed by grouping the equations per node.

- In structured matrices, such as those from partial differential equations on regular grids, a partitioning can be based on the physical domain. Examples are a partitioning along lines in the 2D case, or planes in the 3D case. This will be discussed further in §3.4.3.

- On parallel computers it is natural to let the partitioning coincide with the division of variables over the processors.

3.2.2   Discussion

Jacobi preconditioners need very little storage, even in the block case, and they are easy to implement. Additionally, on parallel computers they don't present any particular problems.

On the other hand, more sophisticated preconditioners usually yield a larger improvement.[1]

3.3   SSOR preconditioning

The SSOR preconditioner[2] like the Jacobi preconditioner, can be derived from the coefficient matrix without any work.

If the original, symmetric, matrix is decomposed as

$$A = D + L + L^T$$

in its diagonal, lower, and upper triangular part, the SSOR matrix is defined as

---

[1]Under certain conditions, one can show that the point Jacobi algorithm is optimal, or close to optimal, in the sense of reducing the condition number, among all preconditioners of diagonal form. This was shown by Forsythe and Strauss for matrices with Property A [96], and by van der Sluis [193] for general sparse matrices. For extensions to block Jacobi preconditioners, see Demmel [63] and Elsner [91].

[2]The SOR and Gauss-Seidel matrices are never used as preconditioners, for a rather technical reason. SOR-preconditioning with optimal ω maps the eigenvalues of the coefficient matrix to a circle in the complex plane; see Hageman and Young [119, §9.3]. In this case no polynomial acceleration is possible, i.e., the accelerating polynomial reduces to the trivial polynomial $P_n(x) = x^n$, and the resulting method is simply the stationary SOR method. Recent research by Eiermann and Varga [81] has shown that polynomial acceleration of SOR with suboptimal ω will yield no improvement over simple SOR with optimal ω.

$$M = (D + L)D^{-1}(D + L)^T,$$

or, parametrized by ω

$$M(\omega) = \frac{1}{2 - \omega}(\frac{1}{\omega}D + L)(\frac{1}{\omega}D)^{-1}(\frac{1}{\omega}D + L)^T.$$

The optimal value of the ω parameter, like the parameter in the SOR method, will reduce the number of iterations to a lower order. Specifically, the spectral condition number $\kappa(M_{\omega_{opt}}^{-1}A) = O(\sqrt{\kappa(A)})$ is attainable, see Axelsson and Barker [14, §1.4]. In practice, however, the spectral information needed to calculate the optimal ω is prohibitively expensive to compute.

The SSOR matrix is given in factored form, so this preconditioner shares many properties of other factorization-based methods (see below). For instance, its suitability for vector processors or parallel architectures depends strongly on the ordering of the variables. On the other hand, since this factorization is given *a priori*, there is no possibility of breakdown as in the construction phase of incomplete factorization methods.

3.4   Incomplete Factorization Preconditioners

A broad class of preconditioners is based on incomplete factorizations of the coefficient matrix. We call a factorization incomplete if during the factorization process certain *fill* elements, zero positions that would be nonzero in an exact factorization, have been ignored. Such a preconditioner is then given in factored form $M = LU$ with L lower and U upper triangular. The efficacy of the preconditioner depends on how well M approximates A.

3.4.1   Creating an incomplete factorization

Incomplete factorizations are the first preconditioners we have encountered so far for which there is a non-trivial creation stage. Incomplete factorizations may break down (attempted division by zero pivot) or result in indefinite matrices (negative pivots) even if the full factorization of the same matrix is guaranteed to exist and yield a positive definite matrix.

An incomplete factorization is guaranteed to exist for many factorization strategies if the original matrix is an M-matrix. This was originally proved by Meijerink and Van der Vorst [149]; see further Beauwens and Quenon [32], Manteuffel [144], and Van der Vorst [195].

In cases where pivots are zero or negative, strategies have been proposed such as substituting an arbitrary positive number (see Kershaw [132]), or restarting the factorization on $A + \alpha I$ for some positive value of α (see Manteuffel [144]).

An important consideration for incomplete factorization preconditioners is the cost of the factorization process. Even if the incomplete factorization exists, the number of operations involved in creating it is at least as much as for solving a system with such a coefficient matrix, so the cost may equal that of one or more iterations of the iterative method. On parallel computers this problem is aggravated by the generally poor parallel efficiency of the factorization.

Such factorization costs can be amortized if the iterative method takes many iterations, or if the same preconditioner will be used for several linear systems, for instance
in successive time steps or Newton iterations.

3.4.2   Point incomplete factorizations

The most common type of incomplete factorization is based on taking a set S of matrix
positions, and keeping all positions outside this set equal to zero during the factorization. The resulting factorization is incomplete in the sense that fill is supressed.

The set S is usually chosen to encompass all positions (i, j) for which $a_{i,j} \neq 0$.
A position that is zero in A but not so in an exact factorization is called a *fill* position,
and if it is outside S, the fill there is said to be "discarded". Often, S is chosen to
coincide with the set of nonzero positions in A, discarding all fill. This factorization
type is called the $ILU(0)$ factorization: the Incomplete LU factorization of degree
zero[3].

We can describe an incomplete factorization formally as

$$\text{for each } k, i, j > k: \quad a_{i,j} \leftarrow \begin{cases} a_{i,j} - a_{i,k} a_{k,k}^{-1} a_{k,j} & \text{if } (i, j) \in S \\ a_{i,j} & \text{otherwise.} \end{cases}$$

Meijerink and Van der Vorst [149] proved that, if A is an M-matrix, such a factorization
exists for any choice of S, and gives a symmetric positive definite matrix if A is
symmetric positive definite. Guidelines for allowing levels of fill were given by Meijerink
and Van der Vorst in [150].

For the $ILU(0)$ method, the incomplete factorization never alters the nonzero
elements of the original matrix, so that we have the following situation. If the coefficient matrix is split into its diagonal, lower triangular, and upper triangular parts as
$A = D + L + U$, the preconditioner can be written as $M = (D + L)D^{-1}(D + U)$ where
D is the diagonal matrix containing the pivots generated.

Remark: the resulting L and U factors of the preconditioner have only nonzero
elements in the set S, but this fact is in general not true for the preconditioner M
itself.

The fact that the $ILU(0)$ preconditioner contains the off-diagonal parts of the original matrix was used by Eisenstat [87] to derive at a more efficient implementation of
preconditioned CG. This new implementation merges the application of the tridiagonal factors of the matrix and the preconditioner, thereby saving a substantial number
of operations per iteration.

Special cases: central differences

Incomplete factorizations of $ILU(0)$ type are particularly simple if the matrix is derived
from central differences on a Cartesian product grid. As remarked above, we only have
to calculate the pivots of the factorization; other elements in the triangular factors are
equal to off-diagonal elements of A.

In the following we will assume a natural, line-by-line, ordering of the grid points.

---

[3]The zero refers to the fact that only "level zero" fill is permitted, that is, nonzero elements of the
original matrix. Fill levels are defined by calling an element of level $k + 1$ if it is caused by elements
at least one of which is of level k. The first fill level is that caused by the original matrix elements.

Letting i,j be coordinates in a regular 2D grid, it is easy to see that the pivot on grid point (i,j) is only determined by pivots on points $(i-1,j)$ and $(i,j-1)$. If there are n points on each of m grid lines, we get the following generating relations for the pivots:

$$
d_{i,i} = \begin{cases}
a_{1,1} & \text{if } i = 1 \\
a_{i,i} - a_{i,i-1}d_{i-1}^{-1}a_{i-1,i} & \text{if } 1 < i \le n \\
a_{i,i} - a_{i,i-n}d_{i-n}^{-1}a_{i-n,i} & \text{if } i = kn+1 \text{ with } k > 1 \\
\begin{aligned} a_{i,i} \quad &- \quad a_{i,i-1}d_{i-1}^{-1}a_{i-1,i} \\ &- a_{i,i-n}d_{i-n}^{-1}a_{i-n,i} \end{aligned} & \text{otherwise.}
\end{cases}
$$

Conversely, we can describe the factorization algorithmically as

Initially: $d_{i,i} = a_{i,i}$ for all i
for $i = 1..nm$ do:
$$
\begin{cases}
d_{i+1,i+1} = d_{i+1,i+1} - a_{i+1,i}d_{i,i}^{-1}a_{i,i+1} & \begin{aligned}&\text{if there is no } k \\ &\text{such that } i = kn\end{aligned} \\
d_{i+n,i+n} = d_{i+n,i+n} - a_{i+n,i}d_{i,i}^{-1}a_{i,i+n} & \text{if } i+n \le nm
\end{cases}
$$

In the above we have assumed that the variables in the problem are ordered according to the so-called "natural ordering": a sequential numbering of the grid lines and the points within each grid line. Below we will encounter different orderings of the variables.

Modified incomplete factorizations

One modification to the basic idea of incomplete factorizations is as follows: If the product $a_{i,k}a_{k,k}^{-1}a_{k,j}$ is nonzero, and fill is not allowed in position (i,j), instead of simply discarding this fill quantity subtract it from diagonal element $a_{i,i}$.

Mathematically this corresponds to forcing the preconditioner to have the same rowsums as the original matrix; in applications of computational fluid mechanics this idea is justified with the argument that the preconditioner does not introduce any artificial diffusion into the system; see Appleyard and Cheshire [4] and Dupont, Kendall and Rachford [78] for early applications of this idea.

Such a factorization scheme is usually called a "modified incomplete factorization". In this case there is a danger of breakdown, especially when the variables are numbered other than in the natural row-by-row ordering. This was noted by Chan and Kuo [49], and a full analysis was given by Eijkhout [83] and Notay [157].

One reason for considering modified incomplete factorizations is the behavior of the spectral condition number of the preconditioned system. It was mentioned above that the condition number of the coefficient matrix is $O(h^{-2})$ as a function of the discretization mesh width. This order of magnitude is preserved by simple incomplete factorizations, although usually a reduction by a large constant factor is obtained.

Modified factorizations are of interest because, in combination with small perturbations, the spectral condition number of the preconditioned system can be of a lower order. It was first proved by Dupont, Kendall and Rachford [78] that a modified incomplete factorization of $A + O(h^2)D_A$ gives $\kappa(M^{-1}A) = O(h^{-1})$ for the central difference case. More general proofs are given by Gustafsson [111], Axelsson and Barker [14, §7.2], and Beauwens [30,31].

A slight variant of modified incomplete factorizations consists of the class of "relaxed incomplete factorizations". Here the fill is multiplied by a parameter $0 < \alpha < 1$ before it is subtracted from the diagonal; see Ashcraft and Grimes [11], Axelsson and Lindskog [18,19], Chan [43], Eijkhout [83], Notay [158], Stone [190], and Van der Vorst [199]. For the dangers of MILU in the presence of rounding error, see Van der Vorst [201].

Parallelism aspects

At first it may appear that the sequential time of solving a factorization is of the order of the number of variables, but things are not quite that bad. Consider the special case of central differences on a regular domain of $n \times n$ points. The variables on any diagonal, that is, in locations (i, j) with $i + j = k$, depend only on those on the previous diagonal, that is, with $i + j = k - 1$. Therefore it is possible to have a vector computer *pipeline* the operations on each diagonal, and a parallel computer can process the elements of a diagonal simultaneously; see Van der Vorst [198,200].

Another way of vectorizing the solution of the triangular factors is to use some expansion. If the lower triangular factor is normalized to the form $I - L$ (where L is strictly lower triangular), then its inverse can be given as either of the following two series:

$$(I - L)^{-1} = \begin{cases} I + L + L^2 + L^3 + \cdots \\ (I + L)(I + L^2)(I + L^4) \cdots \end{cases}$$

(The first series is called a "Neumann expansion", the second an "Euler expansion". Both series are finite, but their length prohibits practical use of this fact.) Parallel or vectorizable preconditioners can be derived from an incomplete factorization by taking a small number of terms in either series. Experiments indicate that a small number of terms, while giving high execution rates, yields almost the full precision of the more recursive triangular solution (see Axelsson and Eijkhout [15] and Van der Vorst [196]).

More radical approaches for increasing the parallelism in incomplete factorizations are based on a renumbering of the problem variables. For instance, on rectangular domains one could start numbering the variables from all four corners simultaneously, thereby creating four-fold parallelism (see Dongarra, *et al.* [68], Van der Vorst [197, 199]). The most extreme case is the red/black ordering (or for more general matrices the multi-color ordering) which gives the absolute minimum number of sequential steps.

Multi-coloring is also an attractive method for vector computers. Since points of one color are uncoupled, they can be processed as one vector; see Doi [65], Melhem [151], and Poole and Ortega [171].

However, for such ordering strategies there is usually a trade-off between the degree of parallelism and the resulting number of iterations. The reason for this is that a different ordering may give rise to a different error matrix, in particular the norm of the error matrix may vary considerably between orderings. See experimental results by Duff and Meurant [76] and a partial explanation of them by Eijkhout [82].

3.4.3   Block factorization methods

We can also consider block variants of preconditioners for accelerated methods. Block methods are normally feasible if the problem domain is a Cartesian product grid; in that case a natural division in lines (or planes in the 3-dimensional case), can be used for blocking, though incomplete factorizations are not as effective in the 3-dimensional case; see for instance Kettler [134]. In such a blocking scheme for Cartesian product grids, both the size and number of the blocks increases with the overall problem size. Another type of block method will be mentioned in §3.4.3.

The idea behind block factorizations

The starting point for an incomplete block factorization is a partitioning of the matrix, as mentioned in §3.2.1. Then an incomplete factorization is performed using the matrix blocks as basic entities (see Axelsson [12] and Concus, Golub and Meurant [55] as basic references).

The most important difference with point methods arises in the inversion of the pivot blocks. Whereas inverting a scalar is easily done, in the block case two problems arise. First, inverting the pivot block is likely to be a costly operation. Second, initially all diagonal blocks of the matrix may be sparse and we would like to maintain this type of structure. Hence the need for approximations of inverses arises.

As in the case of incomplete point factorizations, the existence of incomplete block methods is guaranteed if the coefficient matrix is an M-matrix. For a general proof, see Axelsson [13].

Approximate inverses

In block factorizations a pivot block is generally forced to be sparse, typically of banded form, and that we need an approximation to its inverse that has a similar structure. Furthermore, this approximation should be easily computable, so we rule out the option of calculating the full inverse and taking a banded part of it.

The simplest approximation to A^{-1} is the diagonal matrix D of the reciprocals of the diagonal of A: $d_{i,i} = 1/a_{i,i}$.

Other possibilities were considered by Axelsson and Eijkhout [15], Axelsson and Polman [20], and Concus, Golub and Meurant [55].

Banded approximations to the inverse of banded matrices have a theoretical justification. In the context of partial differential equations the diagonal blocks of the coefficient matrix are usually strongly diagonally dominant. For such matrices, the elements of the inverse have a size that is exponentially decreasing in their distance from the main diagonal. See Demko, Moss and Smith [62] for a general proof, and Eijkhout and Polman [86] for a more detailed analysis in the M-matrix case.

The special case of block tridiagonality

In many applications, a block tridiagonal structure can be found in the coefficient matrix. Examples are problems on a 2D regular grid if the blocks correspond to lines of grid points, and problems on a regular 3D grid, if the blocks correspond to planes of grid points. Even if such a block tridiagonal structure does not arise naturally, it can be imposed by renumbering the variables in a Cuthill-McKee ordering [57].

Such a matrix has incomplete block factorizations of a particularly simple nature: since no fill can occur outside the diagonal blocks ($A_{i,i}$), all properties follow from our treatment of the pivot blocks. The generating recurrence for the pivot blocks also takes a simple form. Let A be the coefficient matrix, block indexed, and let $\{X_i\}_{i=1..n}$ be the sequence of pivots, then

$$X_1 = A_{1,1}$$
$$\textbf{for } i \geq 1$$
$$\text{let } Y_i \approx X_i^{-1}$$
$$X_{i+1} = A_{i+1,i+1} - A_{i+1,i}Y_i A_{i,i+1}$$

The sequence $\{Y_i\}_{i=1..n}$ consists of approximations to the inverses of the pivots in the manner outlined above.

Two types of incomplete block factorizations

One reason that block methods are of interest is that they are potentially more suitable for vector computers and parallel architectures. Consider the block factorization

$$A = (D + L)D^{-1}(D + U) = (D + L)(I + D^{-1}U)$$

where D is the block diagonal matrix of pivot blocks.[4]

Making the transition to an incomplete factorization we can replace the diagonal of pivots D by either the diagonal of incomplete factorization pivots $X = \text{diag}(X_i)$, or the inverse of $Y = \text{diag}(Y_i)$, the diagonal of approximations to the inverses of the pivots. In the first case we find for the incomplete factorization

$$C = (X + L)(I + X^{-1}U)$$

and in the second case

$$C = (Y^{-1} + L)(I + YU).$$

We see that for factorizations of the first type (which covers all methods in Concus, Golub and Meurant [55]) solving a systems means solving smaller systems with the X_i matrices. For the second type (which was discussed by Meurant [152], Axelsson and Polman [20] and Axelsson and Eijkhout [15]) solving a system with C entails *multiplying* by the Y_i blocks. Therefore, the second type has a much higher potential for vectorizability.

Blocking over systems of partial differential equations

If the physical problem has several variables per grid point, that is, if there are several coupled partial differential equations, it is possible to introduce blocking in a natural way.

Blocking of the equations (which gives a small number of very large blocks) was used by Axelsson and Gustafsson [17] for the equations of linear elasticity, and blocking of the variables per node (which gives many very small blocks) was used by Aarden and Karlsson [1] for the semiconductor equations. A systematic comparison of the two approaches was made by Bank, *et al.* [26].

---

[4]Writing $(I + LD^{-1})(D + U)$ is equally valid, but in practice is harder to implement.

3.4.4   Incomplete LQ factorizations

Saad [180] proposes to construct an incomplete LQ factorization of a general sparse matrix. The idea is to orthogonalize the rows of the matrix by a Gram-Schmidt process (note that in sparse matrices, most rows are typically orthogonal already, so that standard Gram-Schmidt may be not so bad as in general). Saad suggest dropping strategies for the fill-in produced in the orthogonalization process. It turns out that the resulting incomplete L factor can be viewed as the incomplete Choleski factor of the matrix AA^T. Experiments show that using L in a CG process for the normal equations: $L^{-1}AA^TL^{-T}y = b$ is effective for some relevant problems.

3.5   Polynomial preconditioners

So far, we have described preconditioners in only one of two classes: those that approximate the coefficient matrix, and where linear systems with the preconditioner as coefficient matrix are easier to solve than the original system. *Polynomial* preconditioners can be considered as members of the second class of preconditioners: direct approximations of the inverse of the coefficient matrix.

Suppose that the coefficient matrix A of the linear system is normalized to the form $A = I - B$, and that the spectral radius of B is less than one. Using the Neumann series, we can write the inverse of A as $A^{-1} = \sum_{k=0}^{\infty} B^k$, so an approximation may be derived by truncating this infinite series. Since the iterative methods we are considering are already based on the idea of applying polynomials in the coefficient matrix to the initial residual, there are analytic connections between the basic method and polynomially accelerated one.

Dubois, Greenbaum and Rodrigue [74] investigated the relationship between a basic method using a splitting $A = M - N$, and a polynomially preconditioned method with

$$M_p^{-1} = (\sum_{i=0}^{p-1}(I - M^{-1}A)^i)M^{-1}.$$

The basic result is that for classical methods, k steps of the polynomially preconditioned method are exactly equivalent to kp steps of the original method; for accelerated methods, specifically the Chebyshev method, the preconditioned iteration can improve the number of iterations by at most a factor of p.

Although there is no gain in the number of times the coefficient matrix is applied, polynomial preconditioning does eliminate a large fraction of the inner products and update operations, so there may be an overall increase in efficiency.

Let us define a polynomial preconditioner more abstractly as any polynomial $M = P_n(A)$ normalized to $P(0) = 1$. Now the choice of the best polynomial preconditioner becomes that of choosing the best polynomial that minimizes $\|I - M^{-1}A\|$. For the choice of the infinity norm we thus obtain Chebyshev polynomials, and they require estimates of both a lower and upper bound on the spectrum of A. These estimates may be derived from the conjugate gradient iteration itself; see §5.1.

Since an accurate lower bound on the spectrum of A may be hard to obtain, Johnson, Micchelli and Paul [126] and Saad [178] propose least squares polynomials based on several weight functions. These functions only require an upper bound and this is easily computed, using for instance the "Gerschgorin bound" $\max_i \sum_j |A_{i,j}|$;

see [206, §1.4]. Experiments comparing Chebyshev and least squares polynomials can be found in Ashby, Manteuffel and Otto [8].

Application of polynomial preconditioning to symmetric indefinite problems is described by Ashby, Manteuffel and Saylor [9]. There the polynomial is chosen so that it transforms the system into a definite one.

3.6 Preconditioners from properties of the differential equation

A number of preconditioners exist that derive their justification from properties of the underlying partial differential equation. We will cover some of them here (see also §5.5 and §5.4). These preconditioners usually involve more work than the types discussed above, however, they allow for specialized faster solution methods.

3.6.1 Preconditioning by the symmetric part

In §2.3.4 we pointed out that conjugate gradient methods for non-selfadjoint systems require the storage of previously calculated vectors. Therefore it is somewhat remarkable that preconditioning by the symmetric part $(A + A^T)/2$ of the coefficient matrix A leads to a method that does not need this extended storage. Such a method was proposed by Concus and Golub [54] and Widlund [211].

However, solving a system with the symmetric part of a matrix may be no easier than solving a system with the full matrix. This problem may be tackled by imposing a nested iterative method, where a preconditioner based on the symmetric part is used. Vassilevski [207] proved that the efficiency of this preconditioner for the symmetric part carries over to the outer method.

3.6.2 The use of fast solvers

In many applications, the coefficient matrix is symmetric and positive definite. The reason for this is usually that the partial differential operator from which it is derived is self-adjoint, coercive, and bounded (see Axelsson and Barker [14, §3.2]). It follows that for the coefficient matrix A the following relation holds for any matrix B from a similar differential equation:

$$c_1 \leq \frac{x^T A x}{x^T B x} \leq c_2 \quad \text{for all } x,$$

where c_1, c_2 do not depend on the matrix size. The importance of this is that the use of B as a preconditioner gives an iterative method with a number of iterations that does not depend on the matrix size.

Thus we can precondition our original matrix by one derived from a different PDE, if one can be found that has attractive properties as preconditioner. One choice would be to take a matrix from a *separable* PDE. A system involving such a matrix can be solved with various so-called "fast solvers", such as FFT methods, cyclic reduction, or the generalized marching algorithm (see Dorr [72], Swarztrauber [191], Bank [24] and Bank and Rose [27]). For instance, if the original matrix arises from

$$-(a(x,y)u_x)_x - (b(x,y)u_y)_y = f,$$

then the preconditioner can be formed from

$$-(\tilde{a}(x)u_x)_x - (\tilde{b}(y)u_y)_y = f.$$

An extension to the non-self adjoint case is considered by Elman and Schultz [90].

Fast solvers are attractive in that the number of operations they require is (slightly higher than) of the order of the number of variables. Coupled with the fact that the number of iterations in the resulting preconditioned iterative methods is independent of the matrix size, such methods are close to optimal. However, fast solvers are usually only applicable if the physical domain is a rectangle or other Cartesian product structure. (For a domain consisting of a number of such pieces, domain decomposition methods can be used; see §5.4).

3.6.3 Alternating Direction Implicit methods

The Poisson differential operator can be split in a natural way as the sum of two operators:

$$\mathcal{L} = \mathcal{L}_1 + \mathcal{L}_2, \qquad \text{where } \mathcal{L}_1 = -\tfrac{\partial^2}{\partial x^2}, \mathcal{L}_2 = -\tfrac{\partial^2}{\partial y^2}.$$

Now let L_1, L_2 be discretized representations of $\mathcal{L}_1$, $\mathcal{L}_2$. Based on the observation that $L_1 + L_2 = (I + L_1)(I + L_2) - I - L_1 L_2$, iterative schemes such as

$$(1 + \alpha L_1)(1 + \alpha L_2)u^{(m+1)} = [(1 + \beta L_1)(1 + \beta L_2)]\, u^{(m)}$$

with suitable choices of α and β have been proposed.

This *alternating direction implicit*, or *ADI*, method was first proposed as a solution method for parabolic equations. The $u^{(m)}$ are then approximations on subsequent time steps. However, it can also be used for the steady state, that is, for solving elliptic equations. In that case, the $u^{(m)}$ become subsequent iterates; see D'Yakonov [79], Fairweather, Gourlay and Mitchell [93], Hadjidimos [118], and Peaceman and Rachford [169]. Generalization of this scheme to variable coefficients or fourth order elliptic problems is relatively straightforward.

The above method is implicit since it requires systems solutions, and it alternates the x and y (and if necessary z) directions. It is attractive from a practical point of view (although mostly on tensor product grids), since solving a system with, for instance, a matrix $I + \alpha L_1$ entails only a number of uncoupled tridiagonal solutions. These need very little storage over that needed for the matrix, and they can be executed in parallel, or one can vectorize over them.

However, there is a problem of data distribution. For vector computers, either the system solution with L_1 or with L_2 will involve very large strides: if columns of variables in the grid are stored contiguously, only the solution with L_1 will involve contiguous data. For the L_2 the stride equals the number of variables in a column.

On parallel machines the same problem occurs, and it requires a global data transposition in between the L_1 and L_2 system solution.

A theoretical reason that ADI preconditioners are of interest is that they can be shown to be spectrally equivalent to the original coefficient matrix. Hence the number of iterations is bounded independent of the condition number.

Chapter 4

Related Issues

4.1 Complex Systems

Conjugate gradient methods for real symmetric systems can be applied to complex Hermitian systems in a straightforward manner. For non-Hermitian complex systems we distinguish two cases. In general, for any coefficient matrix a CGNE method on the normal equations $A^H A x = A^H b$ is possible, or one can split the system into real and complex parts and use a method such as GMRES on the resulting real nonsymmetric system. However, in certain practical situations the complex system is non-Hermitian but symmetric.

Complex symmetric systems can be solved by a classical conjugate gradient or Lanczos method, that is, with short recurrences, if the complex inner product $(x, y) = \bar{x}^T y$ is replaced by $(x, y) = x^T y$. Like the BiConjugate Gradient method, this method is susceptible to breakdown, that is, it can happen that $x^T x = 0$ for $x \neq 0$. A look-ahead strategy can remedy this in most cases (see Freund [97] and Van der Vorst and Melissen [203]).

4.2 Stopping Criteria

An iterative method produces a sequence $\{x^{(i)}\}$ of vectors converging to the vector x satisfying the $n \times n$ system $Ax = b$. To be effective, a method must decide when to stop. A good stopping criterion should

1. identify when the error $e^{(i)} \equiv x^{(i)} - x$ is small enough to stop,

2. stop if the error is no longer decreasing or decreasing too slowly, and

3. limit the maximum amount of time spent iterating.

For the user wishing to read as little as possible, the following simple stopping criterion will likely be adequate. The user must supply the quantities $maxit$, $\|b\|$, $stop\_tol$, and preferably also $\|A\|$:

- The integer $maxit$ is the maximum number of iterations the algorithm will be permitted to perform.

- The real number $\|A\|$ is a *norm* of A. Any reasonable (order of magnitude) approximation of the absolute value of the largest entry of the matrix A will do.

- The real number $\|b\|$ is a *norm* of b. Again, any reasonable approximation of the absolute value of the largest entry of b will do.

- The real number *stop_tol* measures how small the user wants the *residual* $r^{(i)} = Ax^{(i)} - b$ of the ultimate solution $x^{(i)}$ to be. One way to choose *stop_tol* is as the approximate uncertainty in the entries of A and b relative to $\|A\|$ and $\|b\|$, respectively. For example, choosing *stop_tol* 10^{-6} means that the user considers the entries of A and b to have errors in the range $\pm 10^{-6}\|A\|$ and $\pm 10^{-6}\|b\|$, respectively. The algorithm will compute x no more accurately than its inherent uncertainty warrants. The user should choose *stop_tol* less than one and greater than the machine precision ε.[1]

Here is the algorithm:

> $i = 0$
> **repeat**
> $\quad i = i + 1$
> $\quad$ Compute the approximate solution $x^{(i)}$.
> $\quad$ Compute the residual $r^{(i)} = Ax^{(i)} - b$.
> $\quad$ Compute $\|r^{(i)}\|$ and $\|x^{(i)}\|$.
> **until** $i \geq maxit$ or $\|r^{(i)}\| \leq stop\_tol \cdot (\|A\| \cdot \|x^{(i)}\| + \|b\|)$.

Note that if $x^{(i)}$ does not change much from step to step, which occurs near convergence, then $\|x^{(i)}\|$ need not be recomputed. If $\|A\|$ is not available, the stopping criterion may be replaced with the generally stricter criterion

> **until** $i \geq maxit$ or $\|r^{(i)}\| \leq stop\_tol \cdot \|b\|$.

In either case, the final error bound is $\|e^{(i)}\| \leq \|A^{-1}\| \cdot \|r^{(i)}\|$. If an estimate of $\|A^{-1}\|$ is available, one may also use the stopping criterion

> **until** $i \geq maxit$ or $\|r^{(i)}\| \leq stop\_tol \cdot \|x^{(i)}\|/\|A^{-1}\|$,

which guarantees that the relative error $\|e^{(i)}\|/\|x^{(i)}\|$ in the computed solution is bounded by *stop_tol*.

4.2.1   More Details about Stopping Criteria

Ideally we would like to stop when the magnitudes of entries of the error $e^{(i)} = x^{(i)} - x$ fall below a user-supplied threshold. But $e^{(i)}$ is hard to estimate directly, so we use the *residual* $r^{(i)} = Ax^{(i)} - b$ instead, which is more readily computed. The rest of this section describes how to measure the sizes of vectors $e^{(i)}$ and $r^{(i)}$, and how to bound $e^{(i)}$ in terms of $r^{(i)}$.

We will measure errors using *vector* and *matrix norms*. The most common vector norms are:

---

[1]On a machine with IEEE Standard Floating Point Arithmetic, $\varepsilon = 2^{-24} \approx 10^{-7}$ in single precision, and $\varepsilon = 2^{-53} \approx 10^{-16}$ in double precision.

$$\begin{aligned}
\|x\|_\infty &\equiv \max_j |x_j|, \\
\|x\|_1 &\equiv \textstyle\sum_j |x_j|, \text{ and} \\
\|x\|_2 &\equiv (\textstyle\sum_j |x_j|^2)^{1/2}.
\end{aligned}$$

For some algorithms we may also use the norm $\|x\|_{B,\alpha} \equiv \|Bx\|_\alpha$, where B is a fixed nonsingular matrix and α is one of ∞, 1, or 2. Corresponding to these vector norms are three matrix norms:

$$\begin{aligned}
\|A\|_\infty &\equiv \max_j \textstyle\sum_k |a_{j,k}|, \\
\|A\|_1 &\equiv \max_k \textstyle\sum_j |a_{j,k}|, \text{ and} \\
\|A\|_E &\equiv (\textstyle\sum_{jk} |a_{j,k}|^2)^{1/2},
\end{aligned}$$

as well as $\|A\|_{B,\alpha} \equiv \|BAB^{-1}\|_\alpha$. We may also use the matrix norm $\|A\|_2 = (\lambda_{\max}(AA^T))^{1/2}$, where $\lambda_{\max}$ denotes the largest eigenvalue. Henceforth $\|x\|$ and $\|A\|$ will refer to any mutually consistent pair of the above. ($\|x\|_2$ and $\|A\|_E$, as well as $\|x\|_2$ and $\|A\|_2$, both form mutually consistent pairs.) All these norms satisfy the triangle inequality $\|x + y\| \le \|x\| + \|y\|$ and $\|A + B\| \le \|A\| + \|B\|$, as well as $\|Ax\| \le \|A\| \cdot \|x\|$ for mutually consistent pairs. (For more details on the properties of norms, see Golub and Van Loan [108].)

One difference between these norms is their dependence on dimension. A vector x of length n with entries uniformly distributed between 0 and 1 will satisfy $\|x\|_\infty \le 1$, but $\|x\|_2$ will grow like $\sqrt{n}$ and $\|x\|_1$ will grow like n. Therefore a stopping criterion based on $\|x\|_1$ (or $\|x\|_2$) may have to be permitted to grow proportional to n (or $\sqrt{n}$) in order that it does not become much harder to satisfy for large n.

There are two approaches to bounding the inaccuracy of the computed solution to $Ax = b$. Since $\|e^{(i)}\|$, which we will call the *forward error*, is hard to estimate directly, we introduce the *backward error*, which allows us to bound the forward error. The normwise backward error is defined as the smallest possible value of $\max\{\|\delta A\|/\|A\|, \|\delta b\|/\|b\|\}$ where $x^{(i)}$ is the *exact* solution of $(A + \delta A)x^{(i)} = (b + \delta b)$ (here δA denotes a general matrix, not δ times A; the same goes for δb). The backward error may be easily computed from the *residual* $r^{(i)} = Ax^{(i)} - b$; we show how below. Provided one has some bound on the inverse of A, one can bound the forward error in terms of the backward error via the simple equality

$$e^{(i)} = x^{(i)} - x = A^{-1}(Ax^{(i)} - b) = A^{-1}r^{(i)},$$

which implies $\|e^{(i)}\| \le \|A^{-1}\| \cdot \|r^{(i)}\|$. Therefore, a stopping criterion of the form "stop when $\|r^{(i)}\| \le \tau$" also yields an upper bound on the forward error $\|e^{(i)}\| \le \tau \cdot \|A^{-1}\|$. (Sometimes we may prefer to use the stricter but harder to estimate bound $\|e^{(i)}\| \le \| |A^{-1}| \cdot |r^{(i)}| \|$; see §4.2.3. Here $|X|$ is the matrix or vector of absolute values of components of X.)

The backward error also has a direct interpretation as a stopping criterion, in addition to supplying a bound on the forward error. Recall that the backward error is the smallest change $\max\{\|\delta A\|/\|A\|, \|\delta b\|/\|b\|\}$ to the problem $Ax = b$ that makes $x^{(i)}$ an exact solution of $(A+\delta A)x^{(i)} = b+\delta b$. If the original data A and b have errors from previous computations or measurements, then it is usually not worth iterating until δA and δb are even smaller than these errors. For example, if the machine precision is ε, it is not worth making $\|\delta A\| \le \varepsilon\|A\|$ and $\|\delta b\| \le \varepsilon\|b\|$, because just rounding the entries of A and b to fit in the machine creates errors this large.

Based on this discussion, we discuss some stopping criteria and their properties. The first one we discussed above is

Criterion 1. $\|r^{(i)}\| \leq S_1 \equiv stop\_tol \cdot (\|A\| \cdot \|x^{(i)}\| + \|b\|)$. This is equivalent to asking that the backward error δA and δb described above satisfy $\|\delta A\| \leq stop\_tol \cdot \|A\|$ and $\|\delta b\| \leq stop\_tol \cdot \|b\|$. This criterion yields the forward error bound

$$\|e^{(i)}\| \leq \|A^{-1}\| \cdot \|r^{(i)}\| \leq stop\_tol \cdot \|A^{-1}\| \cdot (\|A\| \cdot \|x^{(i)}\| + \|b\|) \ .$$

The second stopping criterion we discussed, which does not require $\|A\|$, may be much more stringent than Criterion 1:

Criterion 2. $\|r^{(i)}\| \leq S_2 \equiv stop\_tol \cdot \|b\|$. This is equivalent to asking that the backward error δA and δb satisfy $\delta A = 0$ and $\|\delta b\| \leq tol \cdot \|b\|$. One difficulty with this method is that if $\|A\| \cdot \|x\| \gg \|b\|$, which can only occur if A is very ill-conditioned and x nearly lies in the null space of A, then it may be difficult for any method to satisfy the stopping criterion. To see that A must be very ill-conditioned, note that

$$1 \ll \frac{\|A\| \cdot \|x\|}{\|b\|} = \frac{\|A\| \cdot \|A^{-1}b\|}{\|b\|} \leq \|A\| \cdot \|A^{-1}\| \ .$$

This criterion yields the forward error bound

$$\|e^{(i)}\| \leq \|A^{-1}\| \cdot \|r^{(i)}\| \leq stop\_tol \cdot \|A^{-1}\| \cdot \|b\|$$

If an estimate of $\|A^{-1}\|$ is available, one can also just stop when the upper bound on the error $\|A^{-1}\| \cdot \|r^{(i)}\|$ falls below a threshold. This yields the third stopping criterion:

Criterion 3. $\|r^{(i)}\| \leq S_3 \equiv stop\_tol \cdot \|x^{(i)}\|/\|A^{-1}\|$. This stopping criterion guarantees that

$$\frac{\|e^{(i)}\|}{\|x^{(i)}\|} \leq \frac{\|A^{-1}\| \cdot \|r^{(i)}\|}{\|x^{(i)}\|} \leq stop\_tol \ ,$$

permitting the user to specify the desired relative accuracy $stop\_tol$ in the computed solution $x^{(i)}$.

One drawback to Criteria 1 and 2 is that they usually treat backward errors in each component of δA and δb equally, since most norms $\|\delta A\|$ and $\|\delta b\|$ measure each entry of δA and δb equally. For example, if A is sparse and δA is dense, this loss of possibly important structure will not be reflected in $\|\delta A\|$. In contrast, the following stopping criterion gives one the option of scaling each component $\delta a_{j,k}$ and δb_j differently, including the possibility of insisting that some entries be zero. The cost is an extra matrix-vector multiply:

Criterion 4. $S_4 \equiv \max_j(|r^{(i)}|_j/(E \cdot |x^{(i)}| + f)_j) \leq stop\_tol$. Here E is a user-defined
matrix of nonnegative entries, f is a user-defined vector of nonnegative entries,
and $|z|$ denotes the vector of absolute values of the entries of z. If this criterion is
satisfied, it means there are a δA and a δb such that $(A + \delta A)x^{(i)} = b + \delta b$, with
$|\delta a_{j,k}| \leq tol \cdot e_{j,k}$, and $|\delta b_j| \leq tol \cdot f_j$ for all j and k. By choosing E and f, the
user can vary the way the backward error is measured in the stopping criterion.
For example, choosing $e_{j,k} = \|A\|_\infty$ and $f_j = \|b\|_\infty$ makes the stopping criterion
$\|r^{(i)}\|_\infty/(n\|A\|_\infty\|x^{(i)}\|_\infty + \|b\|_\infty)$, which is essentially the same as Criterion 1.
Choosing $e_{j,k} = |a_{j,k}|$ and $f_j = |b_j|$ makes the stopping criterion measure the
componentwise relative backward error, i.e., the smallest relative perturbations
in any component of A and b which is necessary to make $x^{(i)}$ an exact solution.
This tighter stopping criterion requires, among other things, that δA have the
same sparsity pattern as A. Other choices of E and f can be used to reflect
other structured uncertainties in A and b. This criterion yields the forward error
bound

$$\|e^{(i)}\|_\infty \leq \| |A^{-1}| \cdot |r^{(i)}| \| \leq S_4 \cdot \| |A^{-1}|(E|x^{(i)}| + f)\|_\infty$$

where $|A^{-1}|$ is the matrix of absolute values of entries of A^{-1}.

Finally, we mention one more criterion, not because we recommend it, but because it
is widely used. We mention it in order to explain its potential drawbacks:

Dubious Criterion 5. $\|r^{(i)}\| \leq S_5 \equiv stop\_tol \cdot \|r^{(0)}\|$. This commonly used criterion
has the disadvantage of depending too strongly on the initial solution $x^{(0)}$. If
$x^{(0)} = 0$, a common choice, then $r^{(0)} = b$. Then this criterion is equivalent to
Criterion 2 above, which may be difficult to satisfy for any algorithm if $\|b\| \ll$
$\|A\| \cdot \|x\|$. On the other hand, if $x^{(0)}$ is very large and very inaccurate, then $\|r^{(0)}\|$
will be very large and S_5 will be artificially large; this means the iteration may
stop too soon. This criterion yields the forward error bound $\|e^{(i)}\| \leq S_5 \cdot \|A^{-1}\|$.

4.2.2 When $r^{(i)}$ or $\|r^{(i)}\|$ is not readily available

It is possible to design an iterative algorithm for which $r^{(i)} = Ax^{(i)} - b$ or $\|r^{(i)}\|$ is not
directly available, although this is *not* the case for any algorithms in this book. For
completeness, however, we discuss stopping criteria in this case.

For example, if ones "splits" $A = M - N$ to get the iterative method $x^{(i)} =$
$M^{-1}Nx^{(i-1)} + M^{-1}b \equiv Gx^{(i-1)} + c$, then the natural residual to compute is $\hat{r}^{(i)} =$
$x^{(i)} - Gx^{(i)} - c = M^{-1}(Ax^{(i)} - b) = M^{-1}r^{(i)}$. In other words, the residual $\hat{r}^{(i)}$ is the
same as the residual of the *preconditioned* system $M^{-1}Ax = M^{-1}b$. In this case, it is
hard to interpret $\hat{r}^{(i)}$ as a backward error for the original system $Ax = b$, so we may
instead derive a forward error bound $\|e^{(i)}\| = \|A^{-1}M\hat{r}^{(i)}\| \leq \|A^{-1}M\| \cdot \|\hat{r}^{(i)}\|$. Using
this as a stopping criterion requires an estimate of $\|A^{-1}M\|$. In the case of methods
based on splitting $A = M - N$, we have $A^{-1}M = (M - N)^{-1}M = (I - G)^{-1}$, and
$\|A^{-1}M\| = \|(I - G)^{-1}\| \leq 1/(1 - \|G\|)$.

Another example is an implementation of the preconditioned conjugate gradient
algorithm which computes $\|r^{(i)}\|_{M^{-1/2},2} = (r^{(i)T}M^{-1}r^{(i)})^{1/2}$ instead of $\|r^{(i)}\|_2$ (the
implementation in this book computes the latter). Such an implementation could use

the stopping criterion $\|r^{(i)}\|_{M^{-1/2},2}/\|r^{(0)}\|_{M^{-1/2},2} \leq tol$ as in Criterion 5. We may also use it to get the forward error bound $\|e^{(i)}\| \leq \|A^{-1}M^{1/2}\| \cdot \|r^{(i)}\|_{M^{-1/2},2}$, which could also be used in a stopping criterion.

4.2.3   Estimating $\|A^{-1}\|$

Bounds on the error $\|e^{(i)}\|$ inevitably rely on bounds for A^{-1}, since $e^{(i)} = A^{-1}r^{(i)}$. There is a large number of problem dependent ways to estimate A^{-1}; we mention a few here.

When a splitting $A = M - N$ is used to get an iteration

$$x^{(i)} = M^{-1}Nx^{(i-1)} + M^{-1}b = Gx^{(i-1)} + c,$$

then the matrix whose inverse norm we need is $I - G$. Often, we know how to estimate $\|G\|$ if the splitting is a standard one such as Jacobi or SOR, and the matrix A has special characteristics such as Property A. Then we may estimate $\|(I - G)^{-1}\| \leq 1/(1 - \|G\|)$.

When A is symmetric positive definite, and Chebyshev acceleration with adaptation of parameters is being used, then at each step the algorithm estimates the largest and smallest eigenvalues $\lambda_{\max}(A)$ and $\lambda_{\min}(A)$ of A anyway. Since A is symmetric positive definite, $\|A^{-1}\|_2 = \lambda_{\min}^{-1}(A)$.

This adaptive estimation is often done using the *Lanczos algorithm*, which can usually provide good estimates of the largest (rightmost) and smallest (leftmost) eigenvalues of a symmetric matrix at the cost of a few matrix-vector multiplies. For general nonsymmetric A, we may apply the Lanczos method to AA^T or $A^T A$, and use the fact that $\|A^{-1}\|_2 = 1/\lambda_{\min}^{1/2}(AA^T) = 1/\lambda_{\min}^{1/2}(A^T A)$.

It is also possible to estimate $\|A^{-1}\|_\infty$ provided one is willing to solve a few systems of linear equations with A and A^T as coefficient matrices. This is often done with dense linear system solvers, because the extra cost of these systems is $O(n^2)$, which is small compared to the cost $O(n^3)$ of the LU decomposition (see Hager [120], Higham [123] and Anderson, *et al.* [3]). This is not the case for iterative solvers, where the cost of these solves may well be several times as much as the original linear system. Still, if many linear systems with the same coefficient matrix and differing right-hand-sides are to be solved, it is a viable method.

The approach in the last paragraph also lets us estimate the alternate error bound $\|e^{(i)}\|_\infty \leq \| |A^{-1}| \cdot |r^{(i)}| \|_\infty$. This may be much smaller than the simpler $\|A^{-1}\|_\infty \cdot \|r^{(i)}\|_\infty$ in the case where the rows of A are badly scaled; consider the case of a diagonal matrix A with widely varying diagonal entries. To compute $\| |A^{-1}| \cdot |r^{(i)}| \|_\infty$, let R denote the diagonal matrix with diagonal entries equal to the entries of $|r^{(i)}|$; then $\| |A^{-1}| \cdot |r^{(i)}| \|_\infty = \|A^{-1}R\|_\infty$ (see Arioli, Demmel and Duff [5]). $\|A^{-1}R\|_\infty$ can be estimated using the technique in the last paragraph since multiplying by $A^{-1}R$ or $(A^{-1}R)^T = R^T A^{-T}$ is no harder than multiplying by A^{-1} and A^{-T} and also by R, a diagonal matrix.

4.2.4   Stopping when progress is no longer being made

In addition to limiting the total amount of work by limiting the maximum number of iterations one is willing to do, it is also natural to consider stopping when no apparent progress is being made. Some methods, such as Jacobi and SOR, often exhibit nearly monotone linear convergence, at least after some initial transients, so it is easy to recognize when convergence degrades. Other methods, like the conjugate gradient method, exhibit "plateaus" in their convergence, with the residual norm stagnating at a constant value for many iterations before decreasing again; in principle there can be many such plateaus (see Greenbaum and Strakos [109]) depending on the problem. Still other methods, such as CGS, can appear wildly nonconvergent for a large number of steps before the residual begins to decrease; convergence may continue to be erratic from step to step.

In other words, while it is a good idea to have a criterion that stops when progress towards a solution is no longer being made, the form of such a criterion is both method and problem dependent.

4.2.5 Accounting for floating point errors

The error bounds discussed in this section are subject to floating point errors, most of which are innocuous, but which deserve some discussion.

The infinity norm $\|x\|_\infty = \max_j |x_j|$ requires the fewest floating point operations to compute, and cannot overflow or cause other exceptions if the x_j are themselves finite[2]. On the other hand, computing $\|x\|_2 = (\sum_j |x_j|^2)^{1/2}$ in the most straightforward manner can easily overflow or lose accuracy to underflow even when the true result is far from either the overflow or underflow thresholds. For this reason, a careful implementation for computing $\|x\|_2$ without this danger is available (subroutine snrm2 in the BLAS [69] [141]), but it is more expensive than computing $\|x\|_\infty$.

Now consider computing the residual $r^{(i)} = Ax^{(i)} - b$ by forming the matrix-vector product $Ax^{(i)}$ and then subtracting b, all in floating point arithmetic with relative precision ε. A standard error analysis shows that the error $\delta r^{(i)}$ in the computed $r^{(i)}$ is bounded by $\|\delta r^{(i)}\| \leq O(\varepsilon)(\|A\| \cdot \|x^{(i)}\| + \|b\|)$, where $O(\varepsilon)$ is typically bounded by $n\varepsilon$, and usually closer to $\sqrt{n}\varepsilon$. This is why one should not choose *stop_tol* $\leq \varepsilon$ in Criterion 1, and why Criterion 2 may not be satisfied by any method. This uncertainty in the value of $r^{(i)}$ induces an uncertainty in the error $e^{(i)} = A^{-1}r^{(i)}$ of at most $O(\varepsilon)\|A^{-1}\| \cdot (\|A\| \cdot \|x^{(i)}\| + \|b\|)$. A more refined bound is that the error $(\delta r^{(i)})_j$ in the jth component of $r^{(i)}$ is bounded by $O(\varepsilon)$ times the jth component of $|A| \cdot |x^{(i)}| + |b|$, or more tersely $|\delta r^{(i)}| \leq O(\varepsilon)(|A| \cdot |x^{(i)}| + |b|)$. This means the uncertainty in $e^{(i)}$ is really bounded by $O(\varepsilon)\||A^{-1}| \cdot (|A| \cdot |x^{(i)}| + |b|)\|$. This last quantity can be estimated inexpensively provided solving systems with A and A^T as coefficient matrices is inexpensive (see the last paragraph of §4.2.3). Both these bounds can be severe overestimates of the uncertainty in $e^{(i)}$, but examples exist where they are attainable.

4.3 Data Structures

The efficiency of any of the iterative methods considered in previous sections is determined primarily by the performance of the matrix-vector product and the preconditioner solve, and therefore on the storage scheme used for the matrix and the

---

[2]IEEE standard floating point arithmetic permits computations with $\pm\infty$ and NaN, or Not-a-Number, symbols.

preconditioner. Since iterative methods are typically used on sparse matrices, we will review here a number of sparse storage formats. Often, the storage scheme used arises naturally from the specific application problem.

In this section we will review some of the more popular sparse matrix formats that are used in numerical software packages such as ITPACK [138] and NSPCG [161]. After surveying the various formats, we demonstrate how the matrix-vector product and an incomplete factorization solve are formulated using two of the sparse matrix formats.

4.3.1   Survey of Sparse Matrix Storage Formats

If the coefficient matrix A is sparse, large-scale linear systems of the form $Ax = b$ can be most efficiently solved if the zero elements of A are not stored. Sparse storage schemes allocate contiguous storage in memory for the nonzero elements of the matrix, and perhaps a limited number of zeros. This, of course, requires a scheme for knowing where the elements fit into the full matrix.

There are many methods for storing the data (see for instance Saad [182] and Eijkhout [84]). Here we will discuss Compressed Row and Column Storage, Block Compressed Row Storage, Diagonal Storage, Jagged Diagonal Storage, and Skyline Storage.

Compressed Row Storage (CRS)

The Compressed Row and Column (in the next section) Storage formats are the most general: they make absolutely no assumptions about the sparsity structure of the matrix, and they don't store any unnecessary elements. On the other hand, they are not very efficient, needing an indirect addressing step for every single scalar operation in a matrix-vector product or preconditioner solve.

The Compressed Row Storage (CRS) format puts the subsequent nonzeros of the matrix rows in contiguous memory locations. Assuming we have a nonsymmetric sparse matrix A, we create 3 vectors: one for floating-point numbers (val), and the other two for integers (col_ind, row_ptr). The val vector stores the values of the nonzero elements of the matrix A, as they are traversed in a row-wise fashion. The col_ind vector stores the column indexes of the elements in the val vector. That is, if val(k) $= a_{i,j}$ then col_ind(k) $= j$. The row_ptr vector stores the locations in the val vector that start a row, that is, if val(k) $= a_{i,j}$ then row_ptr(i) $\leq k <$ row_ptr(i + 1). By convention, we define row_ptr(n + 1) $= nnz + 1$, where nnz is the number of nonzeros in the matrix A. The storage savings for this approach is significant. Instead of storing n^2 elements, we need only $2nnz + n + 1$ storage locations.

As an example, consider the nonsymmetric matrix A defined by

$$A = \begin{pmatrix} 10 & 0 & 0 & 0 & -2 & 0 \\ 3 & 9 & 0 & 0 & 0 & 3 \\ 0 & 7 & 8 & 7 & 0 & 0 \\ 3 & 0 & 8 & 7 & 5 & 0 \\ 0 & 8 & 0 & 9 & 9 & 13 \\ 0 & 4 & 0 & 0 & 2 & -1 \end{pmatrix}. \tag{4.1}$$

The CRS format for this matrix is then specified by the arrays {val, col_ind, row_ptr} given below

val	10	-2	3	9	3	7	8	7	3 $\cdots$ 9	13	4	2	-1
col_ind	1	5	1	2	6	2	3	4	1 $\cdots$ 5	6	2	5	6

row_ptr	1	3	6	9	13	17	20

.

If the matrix A is symmetric, we need only store the upper (or lower) triangular portion of the matrix. The trade-off is a more complicated algorithm with a somewhat different pattern of data access.

Compressed Column Storage (CCS)

Analogous to Compressed Row Storage there is Compressed Column Storage (CCS), which is also called the *Harwell-Boeing* sparse matrix format [75]. The CCS format is identical to the CRS format except that the columns of A are stored (traversed) instead of the rows. In other words, the CCS format is the CRS format for A^T.

The CCS format is specified by the 3 arrays {val, row_ind, col_ptr}, where row_ind stores the row indices of each nonzero, and col_ptr stores the index of the elements in val which start a column of A. The CCS format for the matrix A in (4.1) is given by

val	10	3	3	9	7	8	4	8	8 $\cdots$ 9	2	3	13	-1
row_ind	1	2	4	2	3	5	6	3	4 $\cdots$ 5	6	2	5	6

col_ptr	1	4	8	10	13	17	20

.

Block Compressed Row Storage (BCRS)

If the sparse matrix A is comprised of square dense blocks of nonzeros in some regular pattern, we can modify the CRS (or CCS) format to exploit such block patterns. Block matrices typically arise from the discretization of partial differential equations in which there are several *degrees of freedom* associated with a grid point. We then partition the matrix in small blocks with a size equal to the number of degrees of freedom, and treat each block as a dense matrix, even though it may have some zeros.

If n_b is the dimension of each block and $nnzb$ is the number of nonzero blocks in the $n \times n$ matrix A, then the total storage needed is $nnz = nnzb \times n_b^2$. The block dimension n_d of A is then defined by $n_d = n/n_b$.

Similar to the CRS format, we require 3 arrays for the BCRS format: a rectangular array for floating-point numbers (val$(1 : nnzb, 1 : n_b, 1 : n_b)$) which stores the nonzero blocks in (block) row-wise fashion, an integer array (col_ind$(1 : nnzb)$) which stores the actual column indices in the original matrix A of the $(1,1)$ elements of the nonzero blocks, and a pointer array (row_blk$(1 : n_d + 1)$) whose entries point to the beginning of each block row in val$(:,:,:)$ and col_ind$(:)$. The savings in storage locations and reduction in indirect addressing for BCRS over CRS can be significant for matrices with a large n_b.

Compressed Diagonal Storage (CDS)

If the matrix A is banded with bandwidth that is fairly constant from row to row, then it is worthwhile to take advantage of this structure in the storage scheme by storing subdiagonals of the matrix in consecutive locations. Not only can we eliminate the vector identifying the column and row, we can pack the nonzero elements in such a way as to make the matrix-vector product more efficient. This storage scheme is particularly useful if the matrix arises from a finite element or finite difference discretization on a tensor product grid.

We say that the matrix $A = (a_{i,j})$ is *banded* if there are nonnegative constants p, q, called the left and right *halfbandwidth*, such that $a_{i,j} \neq 0$ only if $i-p \leq j \leq i+q$. In this case, we can allocate for the matrix A an array val$(1:n,-p:q)$. The declaration with reversed dimensions $(-p:q,n)$ corresponds to the LINPACK band format [70], which unlike CDS, does not allow for an efficiently vectorizable matrix-vector multiplication if $p + q$ is small.

Usually, band formats involve storing some zeros. The CDS format may even contain some array elements that do not correspond to matrix elements at all. Consider the nonsymmetric matrix A defined by

$$A = \begin{pmatrix} 10 & -3 & 0 & 0 & 0 & 0 \\ 3 & 9 & 6 & 0 & 0 & 0 \\ 0 & 7 & 8 & 7 & 0 & 0 \\ 0 & 0 & 8 & 7 & 5 & 0 \\ 0 & 0 & 0 & 9 & 9 & 13 \\ 0 & 0 & 0 & 0 & 2 & -1 \end{pmatrix}. \tag{4.2}$$

Using the CDS format, we store this matrix A in an array of dimension $(6,-1:1)$ using the mapping

$$\text{val}(i, j) = a_{i,i+j}. \tag{4.3}$$

Hence, the rows of the val$(:,:)$ array are

val(:,-1)	0	3	7	8	9	2
val(:, 0)	10	9	8	7	9	-1
val(:,+1)	-3	6	7	5	13	0

Notice the two zeros corresponding to non-existing matrix elements.

A generalization of the CDS format more suitable for manipulating general sparse matrices on vector supercomputers is discussed by Melhem in [151]. This variant of CDS uses a *stripe* data structure to store the matrix A. This structure is more efficient in storage in the case of varying bandwidth, but it makes the matrix-vector product slightly more expensive, as it involves a gather operation.

As defined in [151], a stripe in the $n \times n$ matrix A is a set of positions $S = \{(i,\sigma(i)); \ i \in I \subseteq I_n\}$, where $I_n = \{1,\ldots,n\}$ and σ is a strictly increasing function. Specifically, if $(i,\sigma(i))$ and $(j,\sigma(j))$ are in S, then

$$i < j \rightarrow \sigma(i) < \sigma(j).$$

When computing the matrix-vector product $y = Ax$ using stripes, each $(i, \sigma_k(i))$ element of A in stripe S_k is multiplied with both x_i and $x_{\sigma_k(i)}$ and these products are accumulated in $y_{\sigma_k(i)}$ and y_i, respectively. For the nonsymmetric matrix A defined by

$$A = \begin{pmatrix} 10 & -3 & 0 & 1 & 0 & 0 \\ 0 & 9 & 6 & 0 & -2 & 0 \\ 3 & 0 & 8 & 7 & 0 & 0 \\ 0 & 6 & 0 & 7 & 5 & 4 \\ 0 & 0 & 0 & 0 & 9 & 13 \\ 0 & 0 & 0 & 0 & 5 & -1 \end{pmatrix}, \tag{4.4}$$

the 4 stripes of the matrix A stored in the rows of the val(:,:) array would be

val(:,-1)	0	0	3	6	0	5
val(:, 0)	10	9	8	7	9	-1
val(:,+1)	0	-3	6	7	5	13
val(:,+2)	0	1	-2	0	4	0

Jagged Diagonal Storage (JDS)

The Jagged Diagonal Storage format can be useful for the implementation of iterative methods on parallel and vector processors (see Saad [181]). Like the Compressed Diagonal format, it gives a vector length essentially of the size of the matrix. It is more space-efficient than CDS at the cost of a gather/scatter operation.

A simplified form of JDS, called ITPACK storage or Purdue storage, can be described as follows. In the matrix from (4.4) all elements are shifted left:

$$
\begin{pmatrix}
10 & -3 & 0 & 1 & 0 & 0 \\
0 & 9 & 6 & 0 & -2 & 0 \\
3 & 0 & 8 & 7 & 0 & 0 \\
0 & 6 & 0 & 7 & 5 & 4 \\
0 & 0 & 0 & 0 & 9 & 13 \\
0 & 0 & 0 & 0 & 5 & -1
\end{pmatrix}
\longrightarrow
\begin{pmatrix}
10 & -3 & 1 & \\
9 & 6 & -2 & \\
3 & 8 & 7 & \\
6 & 7 & 5 & 4 \\
9 & 13 & & \\
5 & -1 & &
\end{pmatrix}
$$

after which the columns are stored consecutively. All rows are padded with zeros on the right to give them equal length. Corresponding to the array of matrix elements val(:,:), an array of column indices, col_ind(:,:) is also stored:

val(:, 1)	10	9	3	6	9	5
val(:, 2)	-3	6	8	7	13	-1
val(:, 3)	1	-2	7	5	0	0
val(:, 4)	0	0	0	4	0	0

col_ind(:, 1)	1	2	1	2	5	5
col_ind(:, 2)	2	3	3	4	6	6
col_ind(:, 3)	4	5	4	5	0	0
col_ind(:, 4)	0	0	0	6	0	0

It is clear that the padding zeros in this structure may be a disadvantage, especially if the bandwidth of the matrix varies strongly. Therefore, in the CRS format, we reorder the rows of the matrix decreasingly according to the number of nonzeros per row. The compressed and permuted diagonals are then stored in a linear array. The new data structure is called *jagged diagonals*.

The number of jagged diagonals is equal to the number of nonzeros in the first row, *i.e.*, the largest number of nonzeros in any row of A. The data structure to represent the $n \times n$ matrix A therefore consists of a permutation array (perm(1:n)) which reorders the rows, a floating-point array (jdiag(:)) containing the jagged diagonals in succession, an integer array (col_ind(:)) containing the corresponding column indices indices, and finally a pointer array (jd_ptr(:)) whose elements point to the beginning of each jagged diagonal. The advantages of JDS for matrix multiplications are discussed by Saad in [181].

The JDS format for the above matrix A in using the linear arrays {perm, jdiag, col_ind, jd_ptr} is given below (jagged diagonals are separated by semicolons)

jdiag	1	3	7	8	10	2;	9	9	8 $\cdots$ -1;	9	6	7	5;	13
col_ind	1	1	2	3	1	5;	4	2	3 $\cdots$ 6;	5	3	4	5;	6

perm	5	2	3	4	1	6		jd_ptr	1	7	13	17	

Skyline Storage (SKS)

The final storage scheme we consider is for skyline matrices, which are also called variable band or profile matrices (see Duff, Erisman and Reid [77]). It is mostly of importance in direct solution methods, but it can be used for handling the diagonal blocks in block matrix factorization methods. A major advantage of solving linear systems having skyline coefficient matrices is that when pivoting is not necessary, the skyline structure is preserved during Gaussian elimination. If the matrix is symmetric, we only store its lower triangular part. A straightforward approach in storing the elements of a skyline matrix is to place all the rows (in order) into a floating-point array (val(:)), and then keep an integer array (row_ptr(:)) whose elements point to the beginning of each row. The column indices of the nonzeros stored in val(:) are easily derived and are not stored.

For a nonsymmetric skyline matrix such as the one illustrated in Figure 4.1, we store the lower triangular elements in SKS format, and store the upper triangular elements in a column-oriented SKS format (transpose stored in row-wise SKS format). These two separated *substructures* can be linked in a variety of ways. One approach, discussed by Saad in [182], is to store each row of the lower triangular part and each column of the upper triangular part contiguously into the floating-point array (val(:)). An additional pointer is then needed to determine where the diagonal elements, which separate the lower triangular elements from the upper triangular elements, are located.

4.3.2 Matrix vector products

In many of the iterative methods discussed earlier, both the product of a matrix and that of its transpose times a vector are needed, that is, given an input vector x we want to compute products

$$y = Ax \qquad \text{and} \qquad y = A^T x.$$

We will present these algorithms for two of the storage formats from §4.3: CRS and CDS.

CRS Matrix-Vector Product

The matrix vector product $y = Ax$ using CRS format can be expressed in the usual way:

```
+   x   x
x   +   x   x
x   x   +   x           x
    x   x   +   x   x   x   x
            x   +   x   x   x
        x   x   x   +   x   x
            x   x   +   x           x           x
            x   x   x   +   x   x   x           x
            x   x   x   x   +   x   x           x
                        x   +   x   x   x
                x   x   x   x   +   x   x
                        x   x   +   x               x
                        x   x   x   +   x   x   x
                            x   x   +   x       x
                                    +   x   x
                        x   x   x   +   x
                                        +
```

Figure 4.1: Profile of a nonsymmetric skyline or variable-band matrix.

$$y_i = \sum_j a_{i,j} x_j,$$

since this traverses the rows of the matrix A. For an $n \times n$ matrix A, the matrix-vector multiplication is given by

```
for i = 1, n
    y(i)  = 0
    for j = row_ptr(i), row_ptr(i+1) - 1
        y(i) = y(i) + val(j) * x(col_ind(j))
    end;
end;
```

Since this method only multiplies nonzero matrix entries, the operation count is 2 times the number of nonzero elements in A, which is a significant savings over the dense operation requirement of $2n^2$.

For the transpose product $y = A^T x$ we cannot use the equation

$$y_i = \sum_j (A^T)_{i,j} x_j = \sum_j a_{j,i} x_j,$$

since this implies traversing columns of the matrix, an extremely inefficient operation for matrices stored in CRS format. Hence, we switch indices to

$$\text{for all } j, \text{ do for all } i: \quad y_i \leftarrow y_i + a_{j,i} x_j.$$

The matrix-vector multiplication involving A^T is then given by

```
for i = 1, n
    y(i) =  0
end;
```

```
for j = 1, n
    for i = row_ptr(j), row_ptr(j+1)-1
        y(col_ind(i)) = y(col_ind(i)) + val(i) * x(j)
    end;
end;
```

Both matrix-vector products above have largely the same structure, and both use indirect addressing. Hence, their vectorizability properties are the same on any given computer. However, the first product ($y = Ax$) has a more favorable memory access pattern in that (per iteration of the outer loop) it reads two vectors of data (a row of matrix A and the input vector x) and writes one scalar. The transpose product ($y = A^T x$) on the other hand reads one element of the input vector, one row of matrix A, and both reads and writes the result vector y. Unless the machine on which these methods are implemented has three separate memory paths (*e.g.*, Cray Y-MP), the memory traffic will then limit the performance. This is an important consideration for RISC-based architectures.

CDS Matrix-Vector Product

If the $n \times n$ matrix A is stored in CDS format, it is still possible to perform a matrix-vector product $y = Ax$ by either rows or columns, but this does not take advantage of the CDS format. The idea is to make a change in coordinates in the doubly-nested loop. Replacing $j \rightarrow i + j$ we get

$$y_i \leftarrow y_i + a_{i,j} x_j \quad \Rightarrow \quad y_i \leftarrow y_i + a_{i,i+j} x_{i+j} \ .$$

With the index i in the inner loop we see that the expression $a_{i,i+j}$ accesses the jth diagonal of the matrix (where the main diagonal has number 0).

The algorithm will now have a doubly-nested loop with the outer loop enumerating the diagonals diag=-p,q with p and q the (nonnegative) numbers of diagonals to the left and right of the main diagonal. The bounds for the inner loop follow from the requirement that

$$1 \leq \texttt{i}, \texttt{i} + \texttt{j} \leq n.$$

The algorithm becomes

```
for i = 1, n
    y(i) = 0
end;
for diag = -diag_left, diag_right
    for loc = max(1,1-diag), min(n,n-diag)
        y(loc) = y(loc) + val(loc,diag) * x(loc+diag)
    end;
end;
```

The transpose matrix-vector product $y = A^T x$ is a minor variation of the algorithm above. Using the update formula

$$
\begin{aligned}
y_i \quad \leftarrow \quad & y_i + a_{i+j,i} x_j \\
= \quad & y_i + a_{i+j,i+j-j} x_{i+j}
\end{aligned}
$$

we obtain

```
for i = 1, n
    y(i) = 0
end;
for diag = -diag_right, diag_left
    for loc = max(1,1-diag), min(n,n-diag)
        y(loc) = y(loc) + val(loc+diag, -diag) * x(loc+diag)
    end;
end;
```

The memory access for the CDS-based matrix-vector product $y = Ax$ (or $y = A^T x$) is three vectors per inner iteration. On the other hand, there is no indirect addressing, and the algorithm is vectorizable with vector lengths of essentially the matrix order n. Because of the regular data access, most machines can perform this algorithm efficiently by keeping three base registers and using simple offset addressing.

4.3.3 Sparse Incomplete Factorizations

Efficient preconditioners for iterative methods can be found by performing an incomplete factorization of the coefficient matrix. In this section, we discuss the incomplete factorization of an $n \times n$ matrix A stored in the CRS format. Specifically, we are interested in the simplest type of factorization in which no "fill" is allowed, even if the matrix has a nonzero in the fill position. If we split the matrix as $A = D_A + L_A + U_A$ in diagonal, lower and upper triangular part, then the factorization will be of the form $(D_A + L_A)D_A^{-1}(D_A + U_A)$. In this way, we only need to store a diagonal matrix D containing the pivots of the factorization, and a preconditioner solve code is needed for both

$$LUy = x \qquad \text{and} \qquad (LU)^T y = x.$$

The transpose preconditioner solve is for an iterative method involving a transpose matrix-vector product.

Generating a CRS-based Incomplete Factorization

As noted above, for the factorization we only need to store the pivots, so it suffices to allocate a pivot array of length n (`pivots(1:n)`). In fact, we will store the inverses of the pivots rather than the pivots themselves. This implies that during the system solution no divisions have to be performed.

Additionally, we assume that an extra integer array `diag_ptr(1:n)` has been allocated that contains the column (or row) indices of the diagonal elements in each row, that is, `val(diag_ptr(i))` $= a_{i,i}$.

The factorization begins by copying the matrix diagonal

```
for i = 1, n
    pivots(i) = val(diag_ptr(i))
end;
```

Each elimination step starts by inverting the pivot

```
for i = 1, n
    pivots(i) = 1 / pivots(i)
```

For all nonzero elements $a_{i,j}$ with $j > i$, we next check whether $a_{j,i}$ is a nonzero matrix element, since this is the only element that can cause fill with $a_{i,j}$.

```
for j = diag_ptr(i)+1, row_ptr(i+1)-1
    found = FALSE
    for k = row_ptr(col_ind(j)), diag_ptr(col_ind(j))-1
        if(col_ind(k) = i) then
            found = TRUE
            element = val(k)
        endif
    end;
```

If so, we update $a_{j,j}$.

```
    if (found = TRUE)
        val(diag_ptr(col_ind(j))) = val(diag_ptr(col_ind(j)))
                                - element * pivots(i) * val(j)
    end;
end;
```

CRS-based Factorization Solve

The system $LUy = x$ can be solved in the usual manner by introducing a temporary vector z:

$$Lz = x, \qquad Uy = z.$$

We have a choice between several equivalent ways of solving the system:

$$
\begin{aligned}
LU &= (D + L_A)D^{-1}(D + U_A) \\
&= (I + L_A D^{-1})(D + U_A) \\
&= (D + L_A)(I + D^{-1} U_A) \\
&= (I + L_A D^{-1})D(I + D^{-1} U_A)
\end{aligned}
$$

The first and fourth formulae are not suitable since they require both multiplication and division with D; the difference between the second and third is only one of ease of coding. In this section we use the third formula; in the next section we will use the second for the transpose system solution.

Both halves of the solution have largely the same structure as the matrix vector multiplication.

```
for i = 1, n
    sum =  0
    for j = row_ptr(i), diag_ptr(i)-1
        sum = sum + val(j) * z(col_ind(j))
    end;
    z(i) = pivots(i) * (x(i)-sum)
end;
for i = n, 1, (step -1)
    sum = 0
```

```
    for j = diag(i)+1, row_ptr(i+1)-1
        sum = sum + val(j) * y(col_ind(j))
        y(i) = z(i) - pivots(i) * sum
    end;
end;
```

The temporary vector z can be eliminated by reusing the space for y; algorithmically, z can even overwrite x, but overwriting input data is in general not recommended.

CRS-based Factorization Transpose Solve

Solving the transpose system $(LU)^T y = x$ is slightly more involved. In the usual formulation we traverse rows when solving a factored system, but here we can only access columns of the matrices L^T and U^T (at less than prohibitive cost). The key idea is to distribute each newly computed component of a triangular solve immediately over the remaining right-hand-side.

For instance, if we write a lower triangular matrix as $L = (l_{*1}, l_{*2}, \ldots)$, then the system $Ly = x$ can be written as $x = l_{*1}y_1 + l_{*2}y_2 + \cdots$. Hence, after computing y_1 we modify $x \leftarrow x - l_{*1}y_1$, and so on. Upper triangular systems are treated in a similar manner. With this algorithm we only access columns of the triangular systems. Solving a transpose system with a matrix stored in CRS format essentially means that we access rows of L and U.

The algorithm now becomes

```
for i = 1, n
    x_tmp(i) = x(i)
end;
for i = 1, n
    z(i) = x_tmp(i)
    tmp = pivots(i) * z(i)
    for j = diag_ptr(i)+1, row_ptr(i+1)-1
        x_tmp(col_ind(j)) = x_tmp(col_ind(j)) - tmp * val(j)
    end;
end;

for i = n, 1 (step -1)
    y(i) = pivots(i) * z(i)
    for j = row_ptr(i), diag_ptr(i)-1
        z(col_ind(j)) = z(col_ind(j)) - val(j) * y(i)
    end;
end;
```

The extra temporary x_tmp is used only for clarity, and can be overlapped with z. Both x_tmp and z can be considered to be equivalent to y. Overall, a CRS-based preconditioner solve uses short vector lengths, indirect addressing, and has essentially the same memory traffic patterns as that of the matrix-vector product.

4.4   Parallelism

In this section we discuss aspects of parallelism in the iterative methods discussed in this book.

Since the iterative methods share most of their computational kernels we will discuss these independent of the method. The basic time-consuming kernels of iterative schemes are:

- inner products,

- vector updates,

- matrix–vector products, e.g., $Ap^{(i)}$ (for some methods also $A^T p^{(i)}$),

- preconditioner solves.

We will examine each of these in turn. We will conclude this section by discussing two particular issues, namely computational wavefronts in the SOR method, and block operations in the GMRES method.

4.4.1   Inner products

The computation of an inner product of two vectors can be easily parallelized; each processor computes the inner product of corresponding segments of each vector (local inner products or LIPs). On distributed-memory machines the LIPs then have to be sent to other processors to be combined for the global inner product. This can be done either with an all-to-all send where every processor performs the summation of the LIPs, or by a global accumulation in one processor, followed by a broadcast of the final result. Clearly, this step requires communication.

For shared-memory machines, the accumulation of LIPs can be implemented as a critical section where all processors add their local result in turn to the global result, or as a piece of serial code, where one processor performs the summations.

Overlapping communication and computation

Clearly, in the usual formulation of conjugate gradient-type methods the inner products induce a synchronization of the processors, since they cannot progress until the final result has been computed: updating $x^{(i+1)}$ and $r^{(i+1)}$ can only begin after completing the inner product for α_i. Since on a distributed-memory machine communication is needed for the inner product, we cannot overlap this communication with useful computation. The same observation applies to updating $p^{(i)}$, which can only begin after completing the inner product for β_{i-1}.

Figure 4.2 shows a variant of CG, in which all communication time may be overlapped with useful computations. This is just a reorganized version of the original CG scheme, and is therefore precisely as stable. Another advantage over other approaches (see below) is that no additional operations are required.

This rearrangement is based on two tricks. The first is that updating the iterate is delayed to mask the communication stage of the $p^{(i)^T} A p^{(i)}$ inner product. The second trick relies on splitting the (symmetric) preconditioner as $M = LL^T$, so one first computes $L^{-1} r^{(i)}$, after which the inner product $r^{(i)^T} M^{-1} r^{(i)}$ can be computed as $s^T s$

where $s = L^{-1}r^{(i)}$. The computation of $L^{-T}s$ will then mask the communication stage of the inner product.

$$x^{(-1)} = x^{(0)}= \text{initial guess}; \ r^{(0)} = b - Ax^{(0)};$$
$$p^{(-1)} = 0; \beta_{-1} = 0; \alpha_{-1} = 0;$$
$$s = L^{-1}r^{(0)};$$
$$\rho_0 = (s, s)$$
$$\textbf{for } i = 0, 1, 2, ...$$
$$\quad w^{(i)} = L^{-T}s;$$
$$\quad p^{(i)} = w^{(i)} + \beta_{i-1}p^{(i-1)};$$
$$\quad q^{(i)} = Ap^{(i)};$$
$$\quad \gamma = (p^{(i)}, q^{(i)});$$
$$\quad x^{(i)} = x^{(i-1)} + \alpha_{i-1}p^{(i-1)};$$
$$\quad \alpha_i = \rho_i/\gamma;$$
$$\quad r^{(i+1)} = r^{(i)} - \alpha_i q^{(i)};$$
$$\quad s = L^{-1}r^{(i+1)};$$
$$\quad \rho_{i+1} = (s, s);$$
$$\quad \textbf{if } \|r^{(i+1)}\| \ small \ enough \ \textbf{then}$$
$$\quad\quad x^{(i+1)} = x^{(i)} + \alpha_i p^{(i)}$$
$$\quad\quad \text{quit};$$
$$\quad \textbf{endif}$$
$$\quad \beta_i = \rho_{i+1}/\rho_i;$$
$$\textbf{end};$$

Figure 4.2: A rearrangement of Conjugate Gradient for parallelism

Under the assumptions that we have made, CG can be efficiently parallelized as follows:

1. The communication required for the reduction of the inner product for γ can be overlapped with the update for $x^{(i)}$, (which could in fact have been done in the previous iteration step).

2. The reduction of the inner product for ρ_{i+1} can be overlapped with the remaining part of the preconditioning operation at the beginning of the next iteration.

3. The computation of a segment of $p^{(i)}$ can be followed immediately by the computation of a segment of $q^{(i)}$, and this can be followed by the computation of a part of the inner product. This saves on load operations for segments of $p^{(i)}$ and $q^{(i)}$.

For a more detailed discussion see Demmel, Heath and Van der Vorst [64]. This algorithm can be extended trivially to preconditioners of LDL^T form, and nonsymmetric preconditioners in the Biconjugate Gradient Method.

Fewer synchronization points

Several authors have found ways to eliminate some of the synchronization points induced by the inner products in methods such as CG. One strategy has been to replace one of the two inner products typically present in conjugate gradient-like methods by one or two others in such a way that all inner products can be performed simultaneously. The global communication can then be packaged. A first such method was proposed by Saad [177] with a modification to improve its stability suggested by Meurant [153]. Recently, related methods have been proposed by Chronopoulos and Gear [53], D'Azevedo and Romine [59], and Eijkhout [85]. These schemes can also be applied to nonsymmetric methods such as BiCG. The stability of such methods is discussed by D'Azevedo, Eijkhout and Romine [58].

Another approach is to generate a number of successive Krylov vectors (see §2.3.4) and orthogonalize these as a block (see Van Rosendale [205], and Chronopoulos and Gear [53]).

4.4.2   Vector updates

Vector updates are trivially parallelizable: each processor updates its own segment.

4.4.3   Matrix-vector products

The matrix–vector products are often easily parallelized on shared-memory machines by splitting the matrix in strips corresponding to the vector segments. Each processor then computes the matrix–vector product of one strip. For distributed-memory machines, there may be a problem if each processor has only a segment of the vector in its memory. Depending on the bandwidth of the matrix, we may need communication for other elements of the vector, which may lead to communication bottlenecks. However, many sparse matrix problems arise from a network in which only nearby nodes are connected. For example, matrices stemming from finite difference or finite element problems typically involve only local connections: matrix element $a_{i,j}$ is nonzero only if variables i and j are physically close. In such a case, it seems natural to subdivide the network, or grid, into suitable blocks and to distribute them over the processors. When computing Ap_i, each processor requires the values of p_i at some nodes in neighboring blocks. If the number of connections to these neighboring blocks is small compared to the number of internal nodes, then the communication time can be overlapped with computational work. For more detailed discussions on implementation aspects for distributed memory systems, see de Sturler [60] and Pommerell [170].

4.4.4   Preconditioning

Preconditioning is often the most problematic part of parallelizing an iterative method. We will mention a number of approaches to obtaining parallelism in preconditioning.

Discovering parallelism in sequential preconditioners.   Certain preconditioners were not developed with parallelism in mind, but they can be executed in parallel. Some examples are domain decomposition methods (see §5.4), which provide a high degree of coarse grained parallelism, and polynomial preconditioners (see §3.5), which have the same parallelism as the matrix-vector product.

Incomplete factorization preconditioners are usually much harder to parallelize: using wavefronts of independent computations (see for instance Paolini and Radicati di Brozolo [166]) a modest amount of parallelism can be attained, but the implementation is complicated. For instance, a central difference discretization on regular grids gives wavefronts that are hyperplanes (see Van der Vorst [198,200]).

More parallel variants of sequential preconditioners. Variants of existing sequential incomplete factorization preconditioners with a higher degree of parallelism have been devised, though they are perhaps less efficient in purely scalar terms than their ancestors. Some examples are: reorderings of the variables (see Duff and Meurant [76] and Eijkhout [82]), expansion of the factors in a truncated Neumann series (see Van der Vorst [196]), various block factorization methods (see Axelsson and Eijkhout [15] and Axelsson and Polman [20]), and multicolor preconditioners.

Multicolor preconditioners have optimal parallelism among incomplete factorization methods, since the minimal number of sequential steps equals the color number of the matrix graphs. For theory and appplications to parallelism see Jones and Plassman [127,128].

Fully decoupled preconditioners. If all processors execute their part of the preconditioner solve without further communication, the overall method is technically a block Jacobi preconditioner (see §3.2.1). While their parallel execution is very efficient, they may not be as effective as more complicated, less parallel preconditioners, since improvement in the number of iterations may be only modest. To get a bigger improvement while retaining the efficient parallel execution, Radicati di Brozolo and Robert [173] suggest that one construct incomplete decompositions on slightly overlapping domains. This requires communication similar to that for matrix–vector products.

4.4.5   Wavefronts in the Gauss-Seidel and Conjugate Gradient methods

At first sight, the Gauss-Seidel method (and the SOR method which has the same basic structure) seems to be a fully sequential method. A more careful analysis, however, reveals a high degree of parallelism if the method is applied to sparse matrices such as those arising from discretized partial differential equations.

We start by partitioning the unknowns in wavefronts. The first wavefront contains those unknowns that (in the directed graph of $D - L$) have no predecessor; subsequent wavefronts are then sets (this definition is not necessarily unique) of successors of elements of the previous wavefront(s), such that no successor/predecessor relations hold among the elements of this set. It is clear that all elements of a wavefront can be processed simultaneously, so the sequential time of solving a system with $D - L$ can be reduced to the number of wavefronts.

Next, we observe that the unknowns in a wavefront can be computed as soon as all wavefronts containing its predecessors have been computed. Thus we can, in the absence of tests for convergence, have components from several iterations being computed simultaneously. Adams and Jordan [2] observe that in this way the natural ordering of unknowns gives an iterative method that is mathematically equivalent to a multi-color ordering.

In the multi-color ordering, all wavefronts of the same color are processed simultaneously. This reduces the number of sequential steps for solving the Gauss-Seidel matrix to the number of colors, which is the smallest number d such that wavefront i contains no elements that are a predecessor of an element in wavefront $i + d$.

As demonstrated by O'Leary [160], SOR theory still holds in an approximate sense for multi-colored matrices. The above observation that the Gauss-Seidel method with the natural ordering is equivalent to a multicoloring cannot be extended to the SSOR method or wavefront-based incomplete factorization preconditioners for the Conjugate Gradient method. In fact, tests by Duff and Meurant [76] and an analysis by Eijkhout [82] show that multicolor incomplete factorization preconditioners in general may take a considerably larger number of iterations to converge than preconditioners based on the natural ordering. Whether this is offset by the increased parallelism depends on the application and the computer architecture.

4.4.6 Blocked operations in the GMRES method

In addition to the usual matrix-vector product, inner products and vector updates, the preconditioned GMRES method (see §2.3.4) has a kernel where one new vector, $M^{-1}Av^{(j)}$, is orthogonalized against the previously built orthogonal set $\{v^{(1)}, v^{(2)},\ldots, v^{(j)}\}$. In our version, this is done using Level 1 BLAS, which may be quite inefficient. To incorporate Level 2 BLAS we can apply either Householder orthogonalization or classical Gram-Schmidt twice (which mitigates classical Gram-Schmidt's potential instability; see Saad [179]). Both approaches significantly increase the computational work, but using classical Gram-Schmidt has the advantage that all inner products can be performed simultaneously; that is, their communication can be packaged. This may increase the efficiency of the computation significantly.

Another way to obtain more parallelism and data locality is to generate a basis $\{v^{(1)}, Av^{(1)}, \ldots, A^m v^{(1)}\}$ for the Krylov subspace first, and to orthogonalize this set afterwards; this is called m-step GMRES(m) (see Kim and Chronopoulos [137]). (Compare this to the GMRES method in §2.3.4, where each new vector is immediately orthogonalized to all previous vectors.) This approach does not increase the computational work and, in contrast to CG, the numerical instability due to generating a possibly near-dependent set is not necessarily a drawback.

Chapter 5

Remaining topics

5.1   The Lanczos Connection

As discussed by Paige and Saunders in [164] and by Golub and Van Loan in [108], it is straightforward to derive the conjugate gradient method for solving symmetric positive definite linear systems from the Lanczos algorithm for solving symmetric eigensystems and vice versa. As an example, let us consider how one can derive the Lanczos process for symmetric eigensystems from the (unpreconditioned) conjugate gradient method.

Suppose we define the $n \times k$ matrix $R^{(k)}$ by

$$R_k = [r^{(0)}, \ r^{(1)}, \ \ldots, \ r^{(k-1)}],$$

and the $k \times k$ upper bidiagonal matrix B_k by

$$B_k = \begin{bmatrix} 1 & -\beta_2 & & \cdots & 0 \\ & 1 & -\beta_3 & & \vdots \\ & & \ddots & \ddots & \ddots & \\ \vdots & & & \ddots & \ddots & -\beta_k \\ 0 & \cdots & & & & 1 \end{bmatrix},$$

where the sequences $\{r^{(k)}\}$ and $\{\beta_k\}$ are defined by the standard conjugate gradient algorithm discussed in §2.3.1. From the equations

$$p^{(j)} = r^{(j-1)} + \beta_j p^{(j-1)}, \ j = 2, \ 3, \ \ldots, \ k \ ,$$

and $p^{(1)} = r^{(0)}$, we have $R_k = P_k B_k$, where

$$P_k = [p^{(1)}, \ p^{(2)}, \ \ldots, \ p^{(k)}].$$

Assuming the elements of the sequence $\{p^{(j)}\}$ are A-conjugate, it follows that

$$\hat{T}_k = R_k^T A R_k = B_k^T \hat{\Lambda}_k B_k$$

is a tridiagonal matrix since

$$
\hat{\Lambda}_k =
\begin{bmatrix}
{p^{(1)}}^T A p^{(1)} & 0 & \cdots & & 0 \\
0 & {p^{(2)}}^T A p^{(2)} & & & \vdots \\
& & \ddots & \ddots & \ddots \\
\vdots & & \ddots & \ddots & 0 \\
0 & \cdots & & 0 & {p^{(k)}}^T A p^{(k)}
\end{bmatrix} .
$$

Since $\operatorname{span}\{p^{(1)},\ p^{(2)},\ \ldots,\ p^{(j)}\} = \operatorname{span}\{r^{(0)},\ r^{(1)},\ \ldots,\ r^{(j-1)}\}$ and since the elements of $\{r^{(j)}\}$ are mutually orthogonal, it can be shown that the columns of $n \times k$ matrix $Q_k = R_k \Delta^{-1}$ form an orthonormal basis for the subspace $\operatorname{span}\{b,\ Ab,\ \ldots,\ A^{k-1}b\}$, where Δ is a diagonal matrix whose ith diagonal element is $\|r^{(i)}\|_2$. The columns of the matrix Q_k are the Lanczos vectors (see Parlett [167]) whose associated projection of A is the tridiagonal matrix

$$
T_k = \Delta^{-1} B_k^T \Lambda_k B_k \Delta^{-1} , \tag{5.1}
$$

where Λ_k is the diagonal matrix whose ith diagonal element is ${p^{(i)}}^T p^{(i)}$. The extremal eigenvalues of T_k approximate those of the matrix A. Hence, the diagonal and subdiagonal elements of T_k in (5.1), which are readily available during iterations of the conjugate gradient algorithm (§2.3.1), can be used to construct T_k after k CG iterations. This allows us to obtain good approximations to the extremal eigenvalues (and hence the condition number) of the matrix A while we are generating approximations, $x^{(k)}$, to the solution of the linear system $Ax = b$.

For a nonsymmetric matrix A, an equivalent nonsymmetric Lanczos algorithm (see Lanczos [139]) would produce a nonsymmetric matrix T_k in (5.1) whose extremal eigenvalues (which may include complex-conjugate pairs) approximate those of A. The nonsymmetric Lanczos method is equivalent to the BiCG method discussed in §2.3.5.

5.2   Block Iterative Methods

The methods discussed so far are all subspace methods, that is, in every iteration they extend the dimension of the subspace generated. In fact, they generate an orthogonal basis for this subspace, by orthogonalizing the newly generated vector with respect to the previous basis vectors.

However, in the case of nonsymmetric coefficient matrices the newly generated vector may be almost linearly dependent on the existing basis. To prevent breakdown or severe numerical error in such instances, methods have been proposed that perform a look-ahead step (see Freund, Gutknecht and Nachtigal [99], Parlett, Taylor and Liu [168], and Freund and Nachtigal [100]).

Several new, unorthogonalized, basis vectors are generated and are then orthogonalized with respect to the subspace already generated. Instead of generating a basis, such a method generates a series of low-dimensional orthogonal subspaces.

If conjugate gradient methods are considered to generate a factorization of a tridiagonal reduction of the original matrix, then look-ahead methods generate a block factorization of a block tridiagonal reduction of the matrix.

Keeping the block size constant throughout the iteration leads to the Block Lanczos algorithm and the Block Conjugate Gradient method (see O'Leary [159]). In fact, one can show that the spectrum of the matrix is effectively reduced by the $n_b - 1$ smallest eigenvalues, where n_b is the block size.

5.3   Reduced System Preconditioning

As we have seen earlier, a suitable preconditioner for CG is a matrix M such that the system

$$M^{-1}Ax = M^{-1}f$$

requires fewer iterations to solve than $Ax = f$ does, and for which systems $Mz = r$ can be solved efficiently. The first property is independent of the machine used, while the second is highly machine dependent. Choosing the best preconditioner involves balancing those two criteria in a way that minimizes the overall computation time. One balancing approach used for matrices A arising from 5-point finite difference discretization of second order elliptic partial differential equations (PDEs) with Dirichlet boundary conditions involves solving a *reduced system*. Specifically, for an $n \times n$ grid, we can use a point red-black ordering of the nodes to get

$$Ax = \begin{bmatrix} D_R & C \\ C^T & D_B \end{bmatrix} \begin{bmatrix} x_R \\ x_B \end{bmatrix} = \begin{bmatrix} f_R \\ f_B \end{bmatrix}, \tag{5.2}$$

where D_R and D_B are diagonal, and C is a well-structured sparse matrix with 5 nonzero diagonals if n is even and 4 nonzero diagonals if n is odd. Applying one step of block Gaussian elimination (or computing the Schur complement; see Golub and Van Loan [108]) we have

$$\begin{bmatrix} I & O \\ -C^T D_R^{-1} & I \end{bmatrix} \begin{bmatrix} D_R & C \\ C^T & D_B \end{bmatrix} \begin{bmatrix} x_R \\ x_B \end{bmatrix} = \begin{bmatrix} I & O \\ -C^T D_R^{-1} & I \end{bmatrix} \begin{bmatrix} f_R \\ f_B \end{bmatrix}$$

which reduces to

$$\begin{bmatrix} D_R & C \\ O & D_B - C^T D_R^{-1} C \end{bmatrix} \begin{bmatrix} x_R \\ x_B \end{bmatrix} = \begin{bmatrix} f_R \\ f_B - C^T D_R^{-1} f_R \end{bmatrix}.$$

With proper scaling (left and right multiplication by $D_B^{-1/2}$), we obtain from the second block equation the reduced system

$$(I - H^T H)y = g, \tag{5.3}$$

where $H = D_R^{-1/2} C D_B^{-1/2}$, $y = D_B^{1/2} x_B$, and $g = D_B^{-1/2}(f_B - C^T D_R^{-1} f_R)$. The linear system (5.3) is of order $n^2/2$ for even n and of order $(n^2 - 1)/2$ for odd n. Once y is determined, the solution x is easily retrieved from y. The values on the black points are those that would be obtained from a red/black ordered SSOR preconditioner on the full system, so we expect faster convergence.

The number of nonzero coefficients is reduced, although the coefficient matrix in (5.3) has nine nonzero diagonals. Therefore it has higher density and offers more data locality. Meier and Sameh [147] demonstrate that the reduced system approach on hierarchical memory machines such as the Alliant FX/8 is over 3 times faster than unpreconditioned CG for Poisson's equation on $n \times n$ grids with $n \geq 250$.

For 3-dimensional elliptic PDEs, the reduced system approach yields a block tridi-agonal matrix C in (5.2) having diagonal blocks of the structure of C from the 2-dimensional case and off-diagonal blocks that are diagonal matrices. Computing the reduced system explicitly leads to an unreasonable increase in the computational com-plexity of solving $Ax = f$. The matrix products required to solve (5.3) would therefore be performed implicitly which could significantly decrease performance. However, as Meier and Sameh show [147], the reduced system approach can still be about 2-3 times as fast as the conjugate gradient method with Jacobi preconditioning for 3-dimensional problems.

5.4   Domain Decomposition Methods

In recent years, much attention has been given to domain decomposition methods for linear elliptic problems that are based on a partitioning of the domain of the physical problem. Since the subdomains can be handled independently, such methods are very attractive for coarse-grain parallel computers. On the other hand, it should be stressed that they can be very effective even on sequential computers.

In this brief survey, we shall restrict ourselves to the standard second order self-adjoint scalar elliptic problems in two dimensions of the form:

$$-\nabla \cdot (a(x,y)\nabla u) = f(x,y) \tag{5.4}$$

where $a(x,y)$ is a positive function on the domain Ω, on whose boundary the value of u is prescribed (the Dirichlet problem). For more general problems, and a good set of references, the reader is referred to the series of proceedings [46,47,48,106,135,172].

For the discretization of (5.4), we shall assume for simplicity that Ω is triangulated by a set T_H of nonoverlapping coarse triangles (subdomains) $\Omega_i, i = 1, ..., p$ with n_H internal vertices. The Ω_i's are in turn further refined into a set of smaller triangles T_h with n internal vertices in total. Here H, h denote the coarse and fine mesh size respectively. By a standard Ritz-Galerkin method using piecewise linear triangular basis elements on (5.4), we obtain an $n \times n$ symmetric positive definite linear system $Au = f$.

Generally, there are two kinds of approaches depending on whether the subdomains overlap with one another (Schwarz methods) or are separated from one another by interfaces (Schur Complement methods, iterative substructuring).

We shall present domain decomposition methods as preconditioners for the linear system $Au = f$ *or* to a reduced (Schur Complement) system $S_B u_B = g_B$ defined on the interfaces in the non-overlapping formulation. When used with the standard Krylov subspace methods discussed elsewhere in this book, the user has to supply a procedure for computing Av or Sw given v or w and the algorithms to be described herein computes $K^{-1}v$. The computation of Av is a simple sparse matrix-vector multiply, but Sw may require subdomain solves, as will be described later.

5.4.1   Overlapping Subdomain Methods

In this approach, each substructure Ω_i is extended to a larger substructure Ω_i' con-taining n_i' internal vertices and all the triangles $T_i' \subset T_h$, within a distance δ from Ω_i, where δ refers to the amount of overlap.

Let A_i', A_H denote the the discretizations of (5.4) on the subdomain triangulation T_i' and the coarse triangulation T_H respectively.

Let R_i^T denote the extension operator which extends (by zero) a function on T_i' to T_h and R_i the corresponding pointwise restriction operator. Similarly, let R_H^T denote the interpolation operator which maps a function on the coarse grid T_H onto the fine grid T_h by piecewise linear interpolation and R_H the corresponding weighted restriction operator.

With these notations, the *Additive Schwarz Preconditioner* K_{as} for the system $Au = f$ can be compactly described as:

$$K_{as}^{-1}v = R_H^T A_H^{-1} R_H v + \sum_{i=1}^{p} R_i^T A'_i{}^{-1} R_i v.$$

Note that the right hand side can be computed using p subdomain solves using the A_i''s, plus a coarse grid solve using A_H, all of which can be computed in parallel. Each term $R_i^T A'_i{}^{-1} R_i v$ should be evaluated in three steps: (1) Restriction: $v_i = R_i v$, (2) Subdomain solves for w_i: $A_i' w_i = v_i$, (3) Interpolation: $y_i = R_i^T w_i$. The coarse grid solve is handled in the same manner.

The theory of Dryja and Widlund [73] shows that the condition number of $K_{as}^{-1} A$ is bounded independently of both the coarse grid size H and the fine grid size h, provided there is "sufficient" overlap between Ω_i and Ω_i' (essentially it means that the ratio δ/H of the distance δ of the boundary $\partial\Omega_i'$ to $\partial\Omega_i$ should be uniformly bounded from below as $h \to 0$.) If the coarse grid solve term is left out, then the condition number grows as $O(1/H^2)$, reflecting the lack of global coupling provided by the coarse grid.

For the purpose of implementations, it is often useful to interpret the definition of K_{as} in matrix notation. Thus the decomposition of Ω into Ω_i''s corresponds to partitioning of the components of the vector u into p overlapping groups of index sets I_i's, each with n_i' components. The $n_i' \times n_i'$ matrix A_i' is simply a principal submatrix of A corresponding to the index set I_i. R_i^T is a $n \times n_i'$ matrix defined by its action on a vector u_i defined on T_i' as: $(R_i^T u_i)_j = (u_i)_j$ if $j \in I_i$ but is zero otherwise. Similarly, the action of its transpose $R_i u$ forms an n_i'-vector by picking off the components of u corresponding to I_i. Analogously, R_H^T is an $n \times n_H$ matrix with entries corresponding to piecewise linear interpolation and its transpose can be interpreted as a weighted restriction matrix. If T_h is obtained from T_H by nested refinement, the action of R_H, R_H^T can be efficiently computed as in a standard multigrid algorithm. Note that the matrices R_i^T, R_i, R_H^T, R_H are defined by their actions and need not be stored explicitly.

We also note that in this algebraic formulation, the preconditioner K_{as} can be extended to any matrix A, not necessarily one arising from a discretization of an elliptic problem. Once we have the partitioning index sets I_i's, the matrices R_i, A_i' are defined. Furthermore, if A is positive definite, then A_i' is guaranteed to be nonsingular. The difficulty is in defining the "coarse grid" matrices A_H, R_H, which inherently depends on knowledge of the grid structure. This part of the preconditioner can be left out, at the expense of a deteriorating convergence rate as p increases. Radicati and Robert [173] have experimented with such an algebraic overlapping block Jacobi preconditioner.

5.4.2   Non-overlapping Subdomain Methods

The easiest way to describe this approach is through matrix notation. The set of vertices of T_h can be divided into two groups. The set of interior vertices I of all Ω_i and the set of vertices B which lies on the boundaries $\bigcup_i \partial\Omega'_i$ of the coarse triangles Ω'_i in T_H. We shall re-order u and f as $u \equiv (u_I, u_B)^T$ and $f \equiv (f_I, f_B)^T$ corresponding to this partition. In this ordering, equation (5.4) can be written as follows:

$$
\left(
\begin{array}{cc}
A_I & A_{IB} \\
A_{IB}^T & A_B
\end{array}
\right)
\left(
\begin{array}{c}
u_I \\
u_B
\end{array}
\right)
=
\left(
\begin{array}{c}
f_I \\
f_B
\end{array}
\right).
\tag{5.5}
$$

We note that since the subdomains are uncoupled by the boundary vertices, $A_I = blockdiagonal(A_i)$ is block-diagonal with each block A_i being the stiffness matrix corresponding to the unknowns belonging to the *interior* vertices of subdomain Ω_i.

By a block LU-factorization of A, the system in (5.5) can be written as:

$$
\left(
\begin{array}{cc}
I & 0 \\
A_{IB}^T A_I^{-1} & I
\end{array}
\right)
\left(
\begin{array}{cc}
A_I & A_{IB} \\
0 & S_B
\end{array}
\right)
\left(
\begin{array}{c}
u_I \\
u_B
\end{array}
\right)
=
\left(
\begin{array}{c}
f_I \\
f_B
\end{array}
\right),
\tag{5.6}
$$

where

$$
S_B \equiv A_B - A_{IB}^T A_I^{-1} A_{IB}
$$

is the Schur complement of A_B in A.

By eliminating u_I in (5.6), we arrive at the following equation for u_B:

$$
S_B u_B = g_B \equiv f_B - A_{IB} A_I^{-1} f_I.
\tag{5.7}
$$

We note the following properties of this Schur Complement system:

1. S_B inherits the symmetric positive definiteness of A.

2. S_B is dense in general and computing it explicitly requires as many solves on each subdomain as there are points on each of its edges.

3. The condition number of S_B is $O(h^{-1})$, an improvement over the $O(h^{-2})$ growth for A.

4. Given a vector v_B defined on the boundary vertices B of T_H, the matrix-vector product $S_B v_B$ can be computed according to $A_B v_B - A_{IB}^T(A_I^{-1}(A_{IB}v_B))$ where A_I^{-1} involves p independent subdomain solves using A_i^{-1}.

5. The right hand side g_B can also be computed using p independent subdomain solves.

These properties make it possible to apply a preconditioned iterative method to (5.7), which is the basic method in the nonoverlapping substructuring approach. We will also need some good preconditioners to further improve the convergence of the Schur system.

We shall first describe the Bramble-Pasciak-Schatz preconditioner [35]. For this, we need to further decompose B into two non-overlapping index sets:

$$
B = E \cup V_H
\tag{5.8}
$$

where $V_H = \bigcup_k V_k$ denote the set of nodes corresponding to the vertices V_k's of T_H, and $E = \bigcup_i E_i$ denote the set of nodes on the edges E_i's of the coarse triangles in T_H, excluding the vertices belonging to V_H.

In addition to the coarse grid interpolation and restriction operators R_H, R_H^T defined before, we shall also need a new set of interpolation and restriction operators for the edges E_i's. Let R_{E_i} be the pointwise restriction operator (an $n_{E_i} \times n$ matrix, where n_{E_i} is the number of vertices on the edge E_i) onto the edge E_i defined by its action $(R_{E_i} u_B)_j = (u_B)_j$ if $j \in E_i$ but is zero otherwise. The action of its transpose extends by zero a function defined on E_i to one defined on B.

Corresponding to this partition of B, S can be written in the block form:

$$S_B = \begin{pmatrix} S_E & S_{EV} \\ S_{EV}^T & S_V \end{pmatrix}. \tag{5.9}$$

The block S_E can again be block partitioned, with most of the subblocks being zero. The diagonal blocks S_{E_i} of S_E are the principal submatrices of S corresponding to E_i. Each S_{E_i} represents the coupling of nodes on interface E_i separating two neighbouring subdomains.

In defining the preconditioner, the action of $S_{E_i}^{-1}$ is needed. However, as noted before, in general S_{E_i} is a dense matrix which is also expensive to compute, and even if we had it, it would be expensive to compute its action (we would need to compute its inverse or a Cholesky factorization). Fortunately, many efficiently invertible approximations to S_{E_i} have been proposed in the literature (see Keyes and Gropp [136]) and we shall use these so-called interface preconditioners for S_{E_i} instead. We mention one specific preconditioner:

$$M_{E_i} = \alpha_{E_i} K^{1/2}$$

where K is an $n_{E_i} \times n_{E_i}$ one dimensional Laplacian matrix, namely a tridiagonal matrix with 2's down the main diagonal and -1's down the two off-diagonals, and α_{E_i} is taken to be some average of the coefficient $a(x, y)$ of (5.4) on the edge E_i. We note that since the eigen-decomposition of K is known and computable by the Fast Sine Transform, the action of M_{E_i} can be efficiently computed.

With these notations, the Bramble-Pasciak-Schatz preconditioner is defined by its action on a vector v_B defined on B as follows:

$$K_{BPS}^{-1} v_B = R_H^T A_H^{-1} R_H v_B + \sum_{E_i} R_{E_i}^T M_{E_i}^{-1} R_{E_i} v_B. \tag{5.10}$$

Analogous to the additive Schwarz preconditioner, the computation of each term consists of the three steps of restriction-inversion-interpolation and is independent of the others and thus can be carried out in parallel.

Bramble, Pasciak and Schatz [35] prove that the condition number of $K_{BPS}^{-1} S_B$ is bounded by $O(1 + \log^2(H/h))$. In practice, there is a slight growth in the number of iterations as h becomes small (*i.e.*, as the fine grid is refined) or as H becomes large (*i.e.*, as the coarse grid becomes coarser).

The $\log^2(H/h)$ growth is due to the coupling of the unknowns on the edges incident on a common vertex V_k, which is not accounted for in K_{BPS}. Smith [187] proposed a *vertex space* modification to K_{BPS} which explicitly accounts for this coupling and therefore eliminates the dependence on H and h. The idea is to introduce further subsets of B called *vertex spaces* $X = \bigcup_k X_k$ with X_k consisting of a small set of vertices on the edges incident on the vertex V_k and adjacent to it. Note that X overlaps with E and V_H. Let S_{X_k} be the principal submatrix of S_B corresponding to X_k, and $R_{X_k}, R_{X_k}^T$ be the corresponding restriction (pointwise) and extension (by zero) matrices. As before, S_{X_k} is dense and expensive to compute and factor/solve but efficiently invertable approximations (some using variants of the $K^{1/2}$ operator defined before) have been developed in the literature (see Chan, Mathew and Shao [50]). We shall let M_{X_k} be such a preconditioner for S_{X_k}. Then Smith's Vertex Space preconditioner is defined by:

$$K_{VS}^{-1} v_B \;=\; R_H^T A_H^{-1} R_H v_B + \sum_{E_i} R_{E_i}^T M_{E_i}^{-1} R_{E_i} v_B$$
$$+ \sum_{X_k} R_{X_k}^T M_{X_k}^{-1} R_{X_k} v_B. \tag{5.11}$$

Smith [187] proved that the condition number of $K_{VS}^{-1} S_B$ is bounded independent of H and h, provided there is sufficient overlap of X_k with B.

5.4.3   Multiplicative Schwarz Methods

As mentioned before, the Additive Schwarz preconditioner can be viewed as an overlapping block Jacobi preconditioner. Analogously, one can define a *multiplicative* Schwarz preconditioner which corresponds to a symmetric block Gauss-Seidel version. That is, the solves on each subdomain are performed sequentially, using the most current iterates as boundary conditions from neighboring subdomains. Even without conjugate gradient acceleration, the multiplicative method can take many fewer iterations than the additive version. However, the multiplicative version is not as parallelizable, although the degree of parallelism can be increased by trading off the convergence rate through multi-coloring the subdomains. The theory can be found in Bramble, *et al.* [36].

Inexact Solves

The exact solves involving A'^{-1}_i, A_i^{-1} and A_H^{-1} in K_{as}, K_{BPS}, K_{VS} can be replaced by inexact solves $\tilde{A}'^{-1}_i, \tilde{A}_i^{-1}$ and $\tilde{A}_H^{-1}$, which can be standard elliptic preconditioners themselves (e.g. multigrid, ILU, SSOR, etc.).

For the Schwarz methods, the modification is straightforward and the *Inexact Solve Additive Schwarz Preconditioner* is simply:

$$\tilde{K}_{as}^{-1} v = R_H^T \tilde{A}_H^{-1} R_H v + \sum_{i=1}^{p} R_i^T \tilde{A}'^{-1}_i R_i v.$$

The Schur Complement methods require more changes to accommodate inexact solves. By replacing A_H^{-1} by $\tilde{A}_H^{-1}$ in the definitions of K_{BPS} and K_{VS}, we can easily obtain inexact preconditioners $\tilde{K}_{BPS}$ and $\tilde{K}_{VS}$ for S_B. The main difficulty is, however, that the evaluation of the product $S_B v_B$ requires exact subdomain solves in A_I^{-1}. One way to get around this is to use an *inner* iteration using $\tilde{A}_i$ as a preconditioner for A_i in order to compute the action of A_I^{-1}. An alternative is to perform the iteration on the larger system (5.5) and construct a preconditioner from the factorization in (5.6) by replacing the terms A_I, S_B by $\tilde{A}_I, \tilde{S}_B$ respectively, where $\tilde{S}_B$ can be either $\tilde{K}_{BPS}$ or $\tilde{K}_{VS}$. Care must be taken to scale $\tilde{A}_H$ and $\tilde{A}_i$ so that they are as close to A_H and A_i as possible respectively — it is not sufficient that the condition number of $\tilde{A}_H^{-1} A_H$ and $\tilde{A}_i^{-1} A_i$ be close to unity, because the scaling of the coupling matrix A_{IB} may be wrong.

Nonsymmetric Problems

The preconditioners given above extend naturally to nonsymmetric A's (*e.g.*, convection-diffusion problems), at least when the nonsymmetric part is not too large. The nice theoretical convergence rates can be retained provided that the coarse grid size H is chosen small enough (depending on the size of the nonsymmetric part of A) (see Cai and Widlund [42]).

Choice of Coarse Grid Size H

Given h, it has been observed empirically (see Gropp and Keyes [110]) that there often exists an optimal value of H which minimizes the total computational time for solving the problem. A small H provides a better, but more expensive, coarse grid approximation, and requires solving more, but smaller, subdomain solves. A large H has the opposite effect. For model problems, the optimal H can be determined for both sequential and parallel implementations (see Chan and Shao [51]). In practice, it may pay to determine a near optimal value of H empirically if the preconditioner is to be re-used many times. However, there may also be geometric constraints on the range of values that H can take.

5.5 Multigrid Methods

Simple iterative methods (such as the Jacobi method) tend to damp out high frequency components of the error fastest (see §2.2.1). This has led people to develop methods based on the following heuristic:

1. Perform some steps of a basic method in order to smooth out the error.

2. Restrict the current state of the problem to a subset of the grid points, the so-called "coarse grid", and solve the resulting projected problem.

3. Interpolate the coarse grid solution back to the original grid, and perform a number of steps of the basic method again.

Steps 1 and 3 are called "pre-smoothing" and "post-smoothing" respectively; by applying this method recursively to step 2 it becomes a true "multigrid" method. Usually the generation of subsequently coarser grids is halted at a point where the number of variables becomes small enough that direct solution of the linear system is feasible.

The method outlined above is said to be a "V-cycle" method, since it descends through a sequence of subsequently coarser grids, and then ascends this sequence in reverse order. A "W-cycle" method results from visiting the coarse grid *twice*, with possibly some smoothing steps in between.

An analysis of multigrid methods is relatively straightforward in the case of simple differential operators such as the Poisson operator on tensor product grids. In that case, each next coarse grid is taken to have the double grid spacing of the previous grid. In two dimensions, a coarse grid will have one quarter of the number of points of the corresponding fine grid. Since the coarse grid is again a tensor product grid, a Fourier analysis (see for instance Briggs [41]) can be used. For the more general case of self-adjoint elliptic operators on arbitrary domains a more sophisticated analysis is needed (see Hackbusch [116], McCormick [145]). Many multigrid methods can be shown to have an (almost) optimal number of operations, that is, the work involved is proportional to the number of variables.

From the above description it is clear that iterative methods play a role in multigrid theory as smoothers (see Kettler [133]). Conversely, multigrid-like methods can be used as preconditioners in iterative methods. The basic idea here is to partition the matrix on a given grid to a 2×2 structure

$$A^{(i)} = \begin{pmatrix} A^{(i)}_{1,1} & A^{(i)}_{1,2} \\ A^{(i)}_{2,1} & A^{(i)}_{2,2} \end{pmatrix}$$

with the variables in the second block row corresponding to the coarse grid nodes. The matrix on the next grid is then an incomplete version of the Schur complement

$$A^{(i+1)} \approx S^{(i)} = A^{(i)}_{2,2} - A^{(i)}_{2,1} A^{(i)^{-1}}_{1,1} A^{(i)}_{1,2}.$$

The coarse grid is typically formed based on a red-black or cyclic reduction ordering; see for instance Rodrigue and Wolitzer [175], and Elman [89].

Some multigrid preconditioners try to obtain optimality results similar to those for the full multigrid method. Here we will merely supply some pointers to the literature: Axelsson and Eijkhout [16], Axelsson and Vassilevski [22,21], Braess [34], Maitre and Musy [142], McCormick and Thomas [146], Yserentant [213] and Wesseling [210].

5.6   Row Projection Methods

Most iterative methods depend on spectral properties of the coefficient matrix, for instance some require the eigenvalues to be in the right half plane. A class of methods without this limitation is that of row projection methods (see Björck and Elfving [33], and Bramley and Sameh [37]). They are based on a block row partitioning of the coefficient matrix

$$A^T = [A_1, \ldots, A_m]$$

and iterative application of orthogonal projectors

$$P_i x = A_i (A_i^T A_i)^{-1} A_i^T x.$$

These methods have good parallel properties and seem to be robust in handling non-symmetric and indefinite problems.

Row projection methods can be used as preconditioners in the conjugate gradient method. In that case, there is a theoretical connection with the conjugate gradient method on the normal equations (see §2.3.3).

Appendix A

Obtaining the Software

A large body of numerical software is freely available 24 hours a day via an electronic service called *Netlib*. In addition to the template material, there are dozens of other libraries, technical reports on various parallel computers and software, test data, facilities to automatically translate FORTRAN programs to C, bibliographies, names and addresses of scientists and mathematicians, and so on. One can communicate with Netlib in one of a number of ways: by email, (much more easily) via an X-window interface called *XNetlib*, or through anonymous ftp (netlib2.cs.utk.edu).

To get started using netlib, one sends a message of the form send index to netlib@ornl.gov. A description of the entire library should be sent to you within minutes (providing all the intervening networks as well as the netlib server are up).

FORTRAN and C versions of the templates for each method described in this book are available from Netlib. A user sends a request by electronic mail as follows:

mail netlib@ornl.gov

On the subject line or in the body, single or multiple requests (one per line) may be made as follows:

send index from linalg

send sftemplates.shar from linalg

The first request results in a return e-mail message containing the index from the library linalg, along with brief descriptions of its contents. The second request results in a return e-mail message consisting of a shar file containing the single precision FORTRAN routines and a README file. The versions of the templates that are available are listed in the table below:

shar filename	contents
sctemplates.shar	Single precision C routines
dctemplates.shar	Double precision C routines
sftemplates.shar	Single Precision Fortran 77 routines
dftemplates.shar	Double Precision Fortran 77 routines
mltemplates.shar	MATLAB routines

Save the mail message to a file called `templates.shar`. Edit the mail header from this file and delete the lines down to and including `<< Cut Here >>`. In the directory containing the shar file, type

```
sh templates.shar
```

No subdirectory will be created. The unpacked files will stay in the current directory. Each method is written as a separate subroutine in its own file, named after the method (*e.g.*, `CG.f`, `BiCGSTAB.f`, `GMRES.f`). The argument parameters are the same for each, with the exception of the required matrix-vector products and preconditioner solvers (some require the transpose matrix). Also, the amount of workspace needed varies. The details are documented in each routine.

Note that the vector-vector operations are accomplished using the `BLAS` [141] (many manufacturers have assembly coded these kernels for maximum performance), although a mask file is provided to link to user defined routines.

The `README` file gives more details, along with instructions for a test routine.

Appendix B

Overview of the BLAS

The BLAS give us a standardized set of basic codes for performing operations on vectors and matrices. BLAS take advantage of the Fortran storage structure and the structure of the mathematical system wherever possible. Additionally, many computers have the BLAS library optimized to their system. Here we use five routines:

1. `SCOPY`: copies a vector onto another vector

2. `SAXPY`: adds vector x (multiplied by a scalar) to vector y

3. `SGEMV`: general matrix vector product

4. `STRMV`: matrix vector product when the matrix is triangular

5. `STRSV`: solves $Tx = b$ for triangular matrix T

The prefix "S" denotes single precision. This prefix may be changed to "D", "C", or "Z", giving the routine double, complex, or double complex precision. (Of course, the declarations would also have to be changed.) It is important to note that putting double precision into single variables works, but single into double will cause errors.

If we define $a_{i,j} = a(i,j)$ and $x_i = x(i)$, we can see what the code is doing:

- `ALPHA = SDOT( N, X, 1, Y, 1 )` computes the inner product of two vectors x and y, putting the result in scalar α.

  The corresponding Fortran segment is

  ```
  ALPHA = 0.0
  DO I = 1, N
     ALPHA = ALPHA  + X(I)*Y(I)
  ENDDO
  ```

- `CALL SAXPY( N, ALPHA, X, 1, Y )` multiplies a vector x of length n by the scalar α, then adds the result to the vector y, putting the result in y.

  The corresponding Fortran segment is

85

```
DO I = 1, N
   Y(I) = ALPHA*X(I) + Y(I)
ENDDO
```

- CALL SGEMV('N', M, N, ONE, A, LDA, X, 1, 1.0E0, B, 1) computes the
  matrix-vector product plus vector $Ax + b$, putting the resulting vector in b.

  The corresponding Fortran segment:

```
DO J = 1, N
   DO I = 1, M
      B(I) = A(I,J)*X(J) + B(I)
   ENDDO
ENDDO
```

This illustrates a feature of the BLAS that often requires close attention. For
example, we will use this routine to compute the residual vector $b - A\hat{x}$, where $\hat{x}$ is
our current approximation to the solution x (merely change the fourth argument
to -1.0E0). Vector b will be overwritten with the residual vector; thus, if we
need it later, we will first copy it to temporary storage. Also, for readability, we
copy b to the residual vector rk.

- CALL STRMV('U', 'N', 'N', N, T, LDA, X, 1) computes the matrix-
  vector product Tx, putting the resulting vector in x, for upper triangular
  matrix T.

  The corresponding Fortran segment is

```
DO J = 1, N
   TEMP = X(J)
   DO I = 1, J
      X(I) = X(I) + TEMP*T(I,J)
   ENDDO
ENDDO
```

Note that the parameters in single quotes are for descriptions such as 'U' for 'UP-
PER TRIANGULAR', 'N' for 'No Transpose'. This feature will be used extensively,
resulting in storage savings (among other advantages).

The variable LDA is critical for addressing the array correctly. LDA is the leading
dimension of the two-dimensional array A, that is, LDA is the *declared* number of rows
of the two-dimensional array A.

Appendix C

Glossary

Adaptive methods Iterative methods that collect information about the coefficient matrix during the iteration process, and use this to speed up convergence.

Backward error The size of perturbations δA of the coefficient matrix and δb of the right hand side of a linear system $Ax = b$, such that the computed iterate $x^{(i)}$ is the solution of $(A + \delta A)x^{(i)} = b + \delta b$.

Band matrix A matrix A for which there are nonnegative constants p, q such that $a_{i,j} = 0$ if $j < i - p$ or $j > i + q$. The two constants p, q are called the left and right halfbandwidth respectively.

Black box A piece of software that can be used without knowledge of its inner workings; the user supplies the input, and the output is assumed to be correct.

BLAS Basic Linear Algebra Subprograms; a set of commonly occurring vector and matrix operations for dense linear algebra. Optimized (usually assembly coded) implementations of the BLAS exist for various computers; these will give a higher performance than implementation in high level programming languages.

Block factorization See: Block matrix operations.

Block matrix operations Matrix operations expressed in terms of submatrices.

Breakdown The occurrence of a zero divisor in an iterative method.

Choleski decomposition Expressing a symmetric matrix A as a product of a lower triangular matrix L and its transpose L^T, that is, $A = LL^T$.

Condition number See: Spectral condition number.

Convergence The fact whether or not, or the rate at which, an iterative method approaches the solution of a linear system. Convergence can be

- Linear: some measure of the distance to the solution decreases by a constant factor in each iteration.
- Superlinear: the measure of the error decreases by a growing factor.

- Smooth: the measure of the error decreases in all or most iterations, though not necessarily by the same factor.

- Irregular: the measure of the error decreases in some iterations and increases in others. This observation unfortunately does not imply anything about the ultimate convergence of the method.

- Stalled: the measure of the error stays more or less constant during a number of iterations. As above, this does not imply anything about the ultimate convergence of the method.

Dense matrix Matrix for which the number of zero elements is too small to warrant specialized algorithms to exploit these zeros.

Diagonally dominant matrix See: Matrix properties

Direct method An algorithm that produces the solution to a system of linear equations in a number of operations that is determined a priori by the size of the system. In exact arithmetic, a direct method yields the true solution to the system. See: Iterative method.

Distributed memory See: Parallel computer.

Divergence An iterative method is said to diverge if it does not converge in a reasonable number of iterations, or if some measure of the error grows unacceptably. However, growth of the error as such is no sign of divergence: a method with irregular convergence behavior may ultimately converge, even though the error grows during some iterations.

Domain decomposition method Solution method for linear systems based on a partitioning of the physical domain of the differential equation. Domain decomposition methods typically involve (repeated) independent system solution on the subdomains, and some way of combining data from the subdomains on the separator part of the domain.

Field of values Given a matrix A, the field of values is the set $\{x^T A x : x^T x = 1\}$. For symmetric matrices this is the range $[\lambda_{\min}(A), \lambda_{\max}(A)]$.

Fill A position that is zero in the original matrix A but not in an exact factorization of A. In an incomplete factorization, some fill elements are discarded.

Forward error The difference between a computed iterate and the true solution of a linear system, measured in some vector norm.

Halfbandwidth See: Band matrix.

Ill-conditioned system A linear system for which the coefficient matrix has a large condition number. Since in many applications the condition number is proportional to (some power of) the number of unknowns, this should be understood as the constant of proportionality being large.

Incomplete factorization A factorization obtained by discarding certain elements during the factorization process ('modified' and 'relaxed' incomplete factorization compensate in some way for discarded elements). Thus an incomplete LU factorization of a matrix A will in general satisfy $A \neq LU$; however, one hopes that the factorization LU will be close enough to A to function as a preconditioner in an iterative method.

Iterate Approximation to the solution of a linear system in any iteration of an iterative method.

Iterative method An algorithm that produces a sequence of approximations to the solution of a linear system of equations; the length of the sequence is not given a priori by the size of the system. Usually, the longer one iterates, the closer one is able to get to the true solution. See: Direct method.

Krylov sequence For a given matrix A and vector x, the sequence of vectors $\{A^i x\}_{i \geq 0}$, or a finite initial part of this sequence.

Krylov subspace The subspace spanned by a Krylov sequence.

LAPACK A mathematical library of linear algebra routine for dense systems solution and eigenvalue calculations.

Lower triangular matrix Matrix A for which $a_{i,j} = 0$ if $j > i$.

LQ factorization A way of writing a matrix A as a product of a lower triangular matrix L and a unitary matrix Q, that is, $A = LQ$.

LU factorization / LU decomposition Expressing a matrix A as a product of a lower triangular matrix L and an upper triangular matrix U, that is, $A = LU$.

M-Matrix See: Matrix properties.

Matrix norms See: Norms.

Matrix properties We call a square matrix A

> **Symmetric** if $a_{i,j} = a_{j,i}$ for all i, j.
>
> **Positive definite** if it satisfies $x^T A x > 0$ for all nonzero vectors x.
>
> **Diagonally dominant** if $a_{i,i} > \sum_{j \neq i} |a_{i,j}|$; the excess amount $\min_i\{a_{i,i} - \sum_{j \neq i} |a_{i,j}|\}$ is called the diagonal dominance of the matrix.
>
> **An M-matrix** if $a_{i,j} \leq 0$ for $i \neq j$, and it is nonsingular with $(A^{-1})_{i,j} \geq 0$ for all i, j.

Message passing See: Parallel computer.

Multigrid method Solution method for linear systems based on restricting and extrapolating solutions between a series of nested grids.

Modified incomplete factorization See: Incomplete factorization.

Natural ordering See: Ordering of unknowns.

Nonstationary iterative method Iterative method that has iteration-dependent coefficients.

Normal equations For a nonsymmetric or indefinite (but nonsingular) system of equations $Ax = b$, either of the related symmetric systems $(A^T Ax = A^T b)$ and $(AA^T y = b;\ x = A^T y)$. For complex A, A^T is replaced with A^H in the above expressions.

Norms A function $f : R^n \to R$ is called a vector norm if

- $f(x) \geq 0$ for all x, and $f(x) = 0$ only if $x = 0$.
- $f(\alpha x) = |\alpha| f(x)$ for all α, x.
- $f(x + y) \leq f(x) + f(y)$ for all x, y.

The same properties hold for matrix norms. A matrix norm and a vector norm (both denoted $\| \cdot \|$) are called a mutually consistent pair if for all matrices A and vectors x

$$\|Ax\| \leq \|A\|\,\|x\|.$$

Ordering of unknowns For linear systems derived from a partial differential equation, each unknown corresponds to a node in the discretization mesh. Different orderings of the unknowns correspond to permutations of the coefficient matrix. The convergence speed of iterative methods may depend on the ordering used, and often the parallel efficiency of a method on a parallel computer is strongly dependent on the ordering used. Some common orderings for rectangular domains are:

- The natural ordering; this is the consecutive numbering by rows and columns.

- The red/black ordering; this is the numbering where all nodes with coordinates (i, j) for which $i + j$ is odd are numbered before those for which $i + j$ is even.

- The ordering by diagonals; this is the ordering where nodes are grouped in levels for which $i + j$ is constant. All nodes in one level are numbered before the nodes in the next level.

For matrices from problems on less regular domains, some common orderings are:

- The Cuthill-McKee ordering; this starts from one point, then numbers its neighbors, and continues numbering points that are neighbors of already numbered points. The Reverse Cuthill-McKee ordering then reverses the numbering; this may reduce the amount of fill in a factorization of the matrix.

- The Minimum Degree ordering; this orders the matrix rows by increasing numbers of nonzeros.

Parallel computer Computer with multiple independent processing units. If the processors have immediate access to the same memory, the memory is said to be shared; if processors have private memory that is not immediately visible to other processors, the memory is said to be distributed. In that case, processors communicate by message-passing.

Pipelining See: Vector computer.

Positive definite matrix See: Matrix properties.

Preconditioner An auxiliary matrix in an iterative method that approximates in some sense the coefficient matrix or its inverse. The preconditioner, or preconditioning matrix, is applied in every step of the iterative method.

Red/black ordering See: Ordering of unknowns.

Reduced system Linear system obtained by eliminating certain variables from another linear system. Although the number of variables is smaller than for the original system, the matrix of a reduced system generally has more nonzero entries. If the original matrix was symmetric and positive definite, then the reduced system has a smaller condition number.

Relaxed incomplete factorization See: Incomplete factorization.

Residual If an iterative method is employed to solve for x in a linear system $Ax = b$, then the residual corresponding to a vector y is $Ay - b$.

Search direction Vector that is used to update an iterate.

Shared memory See: Parallel computer.

Simultaneous displacements, method of Jacobi method.

Sparse matrix Matrix for which the number of zero elements is large enough that algorithms avoiding operations on zero elements pay off. Matrices derived from partial differential equations typically have a number of nonzero elements that is proportional to the matrix size, while the total number of matrix elements is the square of the matrix size.

Spectral condition number The product

$$\|A\|_2 \cdot \|A^{-1}\|_2 = \frac{\lambda_{\max}^{1/2}(A^T A)}{\lambda_{\min}^{1/2}(A^T A)},$$

where $\lambda_{\max}$ and $\lambda_{\min}$ denote the largest and smallest eigenvalues, respectively. For linear systems derived from partial differential equations in 2D, the condition number is proportional to the number of unknowns.

Spectral radius The spectral radius of a matrix A is $\max\{|\lambda(A)|\}$.

Spectrum The set of all eigenvalues of a matrix.

Stationary iterative method Iterative method that performs in each iteration the same operations on the current iteration vectors.

Stopping criterion Since an iterative method computes successive approximations to the solution of a linear system, a practical test is needed to determine when to stop the iteration. Ideally this test would measure the distance of the last iterate to the true solution, but this is not possible. Instead, various other metrics are used, typically involving the residual.

Storage scheme The way elements of a matrix are stored in the memory of a computer. For dense matrices, this can be the decision to store rows or columns consecutively. For sparse matrices, common storage schemes avoid storing zero elements; as a result they involve indices, stored as integer data, that indicate where the stored elements fit into the global matrix.

Successive displacements, method of Gauss-Seidel method.

Symmetric matrix See: Matrix properties.

Template Description of an algorithm, abstracting away from implementational details.

Tune Adapt software for a specific application and computing environment in order to obtain better performance in that case only. itemize

Upper triangular matrix Matrix A for which $a_{i,j} = 0$ if $j < i$.

Vector computer Computer that is able to process consecutive identical operations (typically additions or multiplications) several times faster than intermixed operations of different types. Processing identical operations this way is called 'pipelining' the operations.

Vector norms See: Norms.

C.1   Notation

In this section, we present some of the notation we use throughout the book. We have tried to use standard notation that would be found in any current publication on the subjects covered.

Throughout, we follow several conventions:

- Matrices are denoted by capital letters.

- Vectors are denoted by lowercase letters.

- Lowercase greek letters usually denote scalars.

We define matrix A of dimension $m \times n$ as follows:

$$A = \begin{bmatrix} a_{1,1} & \cdots & a_{1,n} \\ \vdots & & \vdots \\ a_{m,1} & \cdots & a_{m,n} \end{bmatrix} \qquad a_{i,j} \in \mathcal{R}.$$

We define vector x of dimension n as follows:

$$x = \begin{bmatrix} x_1 \\ \vdots \\ x_n \end{bmatrix} \qquad x_i \in \mathcal{R}.$$

Other notation is as follows:

- $I^{n \times n}$ (or simply I if the size is clear from the context) denotes the identity matrix.

- $A = \text{diag}(a_{i,i})$ denotes that matrix A has elements $a_{i,i}$ on its diagonal, and zeros everywhere else.

- $x_i^{(k)}$ denotes the ith element of vector x during the kth iteration

Bibliography

[1] J. AARDEN AND K.-E. KARLSSON, *Preconditioned CG-type methods for solving the coupled systems of fundamental semiconductor equations*, BIT, 29 (1989), pp. 916–937.

[2] L. ADAMS AND H. JORDAN, *Is SOR color-blind?*, SIAM J. Sci. Statist. Comput., 7 (1986), pp. 490–506.

[3] E. ANDERSON, ET. AL., *LAPACK Users Guide*, SIAM, Philadelphia, 1992.

[4] J. APPLEYARD AND I. CHESHIRE, *Nested factorization*, in Reservoir Simulation Symposium of the SPE, 1983. Paper 12264.

[5] M. ARIOLI, J. DEMMEL, AND I. DUFF, *Solving sparse linear systems with sparse backward error*, SIAM J. Matrix Anal. Appl., 10 (1989), pp. 165–190.

[6] W. ARNOLDI, *The principle of minimized iterations in the solution of the matrix eigenvalue problem*, Quart. Appl. Math., 9 (1951), pp. 17–29.

[7] S. ASHBY, *CHEBYCODE: A Fortran implementation of Manteuffel's adaptive Chebyshev algorithm*, Tech. Report UIUCDCS-R-85-1203, University of Illinois, 1985.

[8] S. ASHBY, T. MANTEUFFEL, AND J. OTTO, *A comparison of adaptive Chebyshev and least squares polynomial preconditioning for Hermitian positive definite linear systems*, SIAM J. Sci. Statist. Comput., 13 (1992), pp. 1–29.

[9] S. ASHBY, T. MANTEUFFEL, AND P. SAYLOR, *Adaptive polynomial preconditioning for Hermitian indefinite linear systems*, BIT, 29 (1989), pp. 583–609.

[10] S. F. ASHBY, T. A. MANTEUFFEL, AND P. E. SAYLOR, *A taxonomy for conjugate gradient methods*, SIAM J. Numer. Anal., 27 (1990), pp. 1542–1568.

[11] C. ASHCRAFT AND R. GRIMES, *On vectorizing incomplete factorizations and SSOR preconditioners*, SIAM J. Sci. Statist. Comput., 9 (1988), pp. 122–151.

[12] O. AXELSSON, *Incomplete block matrix factorization preconditioning methods. The ultimate answer?*, J. Comput. Appl. Math., 12&13 (1985), pp. 3–18.

[13] ——, *A general incomplete block-matrix factorization method*, Linear Algebra Appl., 74 (1986), pp. 179–190.

[14] O. AXELSSON AND A. BARKER, *Finite element solution of boundary value problems. Theory and computation*, Academic Press, Orlando, Fl., 1984.

[15] O. AXELSSON AND V. EIJKHOUT, *Vectorizable preconditioners for elliptic difference equations in three space dimensions*, J. Comput. Appl. Math., 27 (1989), pp. 299–321.

[16] ———, *The nested recursive two-level factorization method for nine-point difference matrices*, SIAM J. Sci. Statist. Comput., 12 (1991), pp. 1373–1400.

[17] O. AXELSSON AND I. GUSTAFSSON, *Iterative solution for the solution of the Navier equations of elasticity*, Comput. Methods Appl. Mech. Engrg., 15 (1978), pp. 241–258.

[18] O. AXELSSON AND G. LINDSKOG, *On the eigenvalue distribution of a class of preconditioning matrices*, Numer. Math., 48 (1986), pp. 479–498.

[19] ———, *On the rate of convergence of the preconditioned conjugate gradient method*, Numer. Math., 48 (1986), pp. 499–523.

[20] O. AXELSSON AND B. POLMAN, *On approximate factorization methods for block-matrices suitable for vector and parallel processors*, Linear Algebra Appl., 77 (1986), pp. 3–26.

[21] O. AXELSSON AND P. VASSILEVSKI, *Algebraic multilevel preconditioning methods, I*, Numer. Math., 56 (1989), pp. 157–177.

[22] ———, *Algebraic multilevel preconditioning methods, II*, SIAM J. Numer. Anal., 27 (1990), pp. 1569–1590.

[23] O. AXELSSON AND P. S. VASSILEVSKI, *A black box generalized conjugate gradient solver with inner iterations and variable-step preconditioning*, SIAM J. Matrix Anal. Appl., 12 (1991), pp. 625–644.

[24] R. BANK, *Marching algorithms for elliptic boundary value problems; II: The variable coefficient case*, SIAM J. Numer. Anal., 14 (1977), pp. 950–970.

[25] R. BANK AND T. CHAN, *An analysis of the composite step Bi-conjugate gradient method*, Tech. Report CAM 92-, UCLA, Dept. of Math., Los Angeles, CA 90024-1555, 1992.

[26] R. BANK, T. CHAN, W. COUGHRAN JR., AND R. SMITH, *The Alternate-Block-Factorization procedure for systems of partial differential equations*, BIT, 29 (1989), pp. 938–954.

[27] R. BANK AND D. ROSE, *Marching algorithms for elliptic boundary value problems. I: The constant coefficient case*, SIAM J. Numer. Anal., 14 (1977), pp. 792–829.

[28] R. E. BANK AND T. F. CHAN, *A composite step bi-conjugate gradient algorithm for nonsymmetric linear systems*, Tech. Report CAM 92-, UCLA, Dept. of Math., Los Angeles, CA 90024-1555, 1992.

[29] G. BAUDET, *Asynchronous iterative methods for multiprocessors*, J. Assoc. Comput. Mach., 25 (1978), pp. 226–244.

[30] R. BEAUWENS, *On Axelsson's perturbations*, Linear Algebra Appl., 68 (1985), pp. 221–242.

[31] ———, *Approximate factorizations with S/P consistently ordered M-factors*, BIT, 29 (1989), pp. 658–681.

[32] R. BEAUWENS AND L. QUENON, *Existence criteria for partial matrix factorizations in iterative methods*, SIAM J. Numer. Anal., 13 (1976), pp. 615–643.

[33] A. BJÖRCK AND T. ELFVING, *Accelerated projection methods for computing pseudo-inverse solutions of systems of linear equations*, BIT, 19 (1979), pp. 145–163.

[34] D. BRAESS, *The contraction number of a multigrid method for solving the Poisson equation*, Numer. Math., 37 (1981), pp. 387–404.

[35] J. H. BRAMBLE, J. E. PASCIAK, AND A. H. SCHATZ, *The construction of preconditioners for elliptic problems by substructuring, I*, Mathematics of Computation, 47 (1986), pp. 103–134.

[36] J. H. BRAMBLE, J. E. PASCIAK, J. WANG, AND J. XU, *Convergence estimates for product iterative methods with applications to domain decompositions and multigrid*, Math. Comp., to appear.

[37] R. BRAMLEY AND A. SAMEH, *Row projection methods for large nonsymmetric linear systems*, SIAM J. Sci. Statist. Comput., 13 (1992), pp. 168–193.

[38] C. BREZINSKI AND H. SADOK, *Avoiding breakdown in the CGS algorithm*, Numer. Alg., 1 (1991), pp. 199–206.

[39] C. BREZINSKI, M. ZAGLIA, AND H. SADOK, *Avoiding breakdown and near breakdown in Lanczos type algorithms*, Numer. Alg., 1 (1991), pp. 261–284.

[40] ———, *A breakdown free Lanczos type algorithm for solving linear systems*, Numer. Math., 63 (1992), pp. 29–38.

[41] W. BRIGGS, *A Multigrid Tutorial*, SIAM, Philadelphia, 1977.

[42] X.-C. CAI AND O. WIDLUND, *Multiplicative Schwarz algorithms for some nonsymmetric and indefinite problems*, SIAM J. Numer. Anal., 30 (1993), pp. 936–952.

[43] T. CHAN, *Fourier analysis of relaxed incomplete factorization preconditioners*, SIAM J. Sci. Statist. Comput., 12 (1991), pp. 668–680.

[44] T. CHAN, L. DE PILLIS, AND H. VAN DER VORST, *A transpose-free squared Lanczos algorithm and application to solving nonsymmetric linear systems*, Tech. Report CAM 91-17, UCLA, Dept. of Math., Los Angeles, CA 90024-1555, 1991.

[45] T. CHAN, E. GALLOPOULOS, V. SIMONCINI, T. SZETO, AND C. TONG, *A quasi-minimal residual variant of the Bi-CGSTAB algorithm for nonsymmetric systems*, Tech. Report CAM 92-26, UCLA, Dept. of Math., Los Angeles, CA 90024-1555, 1992. SIAM J. Sci. Comput., to appear.

[46] T. CHAN, R. GLOWINSKI, , J. PÉRIAUX, AND O. WIDLUND, eds., *Domain Decomposition Methods*, Philadelphia, 1989, SIAM. Proceedings of the Second International Symposium on Domain Decomposition Methods, Los Angeles, CA, January 14 - 16, 1988.

[47] ——, eds., *Domain Decomposition Methods*, Philadelphia, 1990, SIAM. Proceedings of the Third International Symposium on Domain Decomposition Methods, Houston, TX, 1989.

[48] ——, eds., *Domain Decomposition Methods*, SIAM, Philadelphia, 1991. Proceedings of the Fourth International Symposium on Domain Decomposition Methods, Moscow, USSR, 1990.

[49] T. CHAN AND C.-C. J. KUO, *Two-color Fourier analysis of iterative algorithms for elliptic problems with red/black ordering*, SIAM J. Sci. Statist. Comput., 11 (1990), pp. 767–793.

[50] T. F. CHAN, T. P. MATHEW, AND J. P. SHAO, *Efficient variants of the vertex space domain decomposition algorithm*, Tech. Report CAM 92-07, UCLA, Dept. of Math., Los Angeles, CA 90024-1555, 1992. SIAM J. Sci. Comput., to appear.

[51] T. F. CHAN AND J. SHAO, *On the choice of coarse grid size in domain decomposition methods*, tech. report, UCLA, Dept. of Math., Los Angeles, CA 90024-1555, 1993. to appear.

[52] D. CHAZAN AND W. MIRANKER, *Chaotic relaxation*, Linear Algebra Appl., 2 (1969), pp. 199–222.

[53] A. CHRONOPOULOS AND C. GEAR, *s-step iterative methods for symmetric linear systems*, J. Comput. Appl. Math., 25 (1989), pp. 153–168.

[54] P. CONCUS AND G. GOLUB, *A generalized conjugate gradient method for nonsymmetric systems of linear equations*, in Computer methods in Applied Sciences and Engineering, Second International Symposium, Dec 15–19, 1975; Lecture Notes in Economics and Mathematical Systems, Vol. 134, Berlin, New York, 1976, Springer-Verlag.

[55] P. CONCUS, G. GOLUB, AND G. MEURANT, *Block preconditioning for the conjugate gradient method*, SIAM J. Sci. Statist. Comput., 6 (1985), pp. 220–252.

[56] P. CONCUS, G. GOLUB, AND D. O'LEARY, *A generalized conjugate gradient method for the numerical solution of elliptic partial differential equations*, in Sparse Matrix Computations, J. Bunch and D. Rose, eds., Academic Press, New York, 1976, pp. 309–332.

[57] E. CUTHILL AND J. MCKEE, *Reducing the bandwidth of sparse symmetric matrices*, in ACM Proceedings of the 24th National Conference, 1969.

[58] E. D'AZEVEDO, V. EIJKHOUT, AND C. ROMINE, *LAPACK working note 56: Reducing communication costs in the conjugate gradient algorithm on distributed memory multiprocessor*, tech. report, Computer Science Department, University of Tennessee, Knoxville, TN, 1993.

[59] E. D'AZEVEDO AND C. ROMINE, *Reducing communication costs in the conjugate gradient algorithm on distributed memory multiprocessors*, Tech. Report ORNL/TM-12192, Oak Ridge National Lab, Oak Ridge, TN, 1992.

[60] E. DE STURLER, *A parallel restructured version of GMRES(m)*, Tech. Report 91-85, Delft University of Technology, Delft, The Netherlands, 1991.

[61] E. DE STURLER AND D. R. FOKKEMA, *Nested Krylov methods and preserving the orthogonality*, Tech. Report Preprint 796, Utrecht University, Utrecht, The Netherlands, 1993.

[62] S. DEMKO, W. MOSS, AND P. SMITH, *Decay rates for inverses of band matrices*, Mathematics of Computation, 43 (1984), pp. 491–499.

[63] J. DEMMEL, *The condition number of equivalence transformations that block diagonalize matrix pencils*, SIAM J. Numer. Anal., 20 (1983), pp. 599–610.

[64] J. DEMMEL, M. HEATH, AND H. VAN DER VORST, *Parallel linear algebra*, in Acta Numerica, Vol. 2, Cambridge Press, New York, 1993.

[65] S. DOI, *On parallelism and convergence of incomplete LU factorizations*, Appl. Numer. Math., 7 (1991), pp. 417–436.

[66] J. DONGARRA, J. DUCROZ, I. DUFF, AND S. HAMMARLING, *A set of level 3 Basic Linear Algebra Subprograms*, ACM Trans. Math. Soft., 16 (1990), pp. 1–17.

[67] J. DONGARRA, J. DUCROZ, S. HAMMARLING, AND R. HANSON, *An extended set of FORTRAN Basic Linear Algebra Subprograms*, ACM Trans. Math. Soft., 14 (1988), pp. 1–32.

[68] J. DONGARRA, I. DUFF, D. SORENSEN, AND H. VAN DER VORST, *Solving Linear Systems on Vector and Shared Memory Computers*, SIAM, Philadelphia, PA, 1991.

[69] J. DONGARRA AND E. GROSSE, *Distribution of mathematical software via electronic mail*, Comm. ACM, 30 (1987), pp. 403–407.

[70] J. DONGARRA, C. MOLER, J. BUNCH, AND G. STEWART, *LINPACK Users' Guide*, SIAM, Philadelphia, 1979.

[71] J. DONGARRA AND H. VAN DER VORST, *Performance of various computers using standard sparse linear equations solving techniques*, in Computer Benchmarks, J. Dongarra and W. Gentzsch, eds., Elsevier Science Publishers B.V., New York, 1993, pp. 177–188.

[72] F. DORR, *The direct solution of the discrete Poisson equation on a rectangle*, SIAM Rev., 12 (1970), pp. 248–263.

[73] M. DRYJA AND O. B. WIDLUND, *Towards a unified theory of domain decomposition algorithms for elliptic problems*, Tech. Report 486, also Ultracomputer Note 167, Department of Computer Science, Courant Institute, 1989.

[74] D. DUBOIS, A. GREENBAUM, AND G. RODRIGUE, *Approximating the inverse of a matrix for use in iterative algorithms on vector processors*, Computing, 22 (1979), pp. 257–268.

[75] I. DUFF, R. GRIMES, AND J. LEWIS, *Sparse matrix test problems*, ACM Trans. Math. Soft., 15 (1989), pp. 1–14.

[76] I. DUFF AND G. MEURANT, *The effect of ordering on preconditioned conjugate gradients*, BIT, 29 (1989), pp. 635–657.

[77] I. S. DUFF, A. M. ERISMAN, AND J.K.REID, *Direct methods for sparse matrices*, Oxford University Press, London, 1986.

[78] T. DUPONT, R. KENDALL, AND H. RACHFORD, *An approximate factorization procedure for solving self-adjoint elliptic difference equations*, SIAM J. Numer. Anal., 5 (1968), pp. 559–573.

[79] E. D'YAKONOV, *The method of variable directions in solving systems of finite difference equations*, Soviet Math. Dokl., 2 (1961), pp. 577–580. TOM 138, 271–274.

[80] L. EHRLICH, *An Ad-Hoc SOR method*, J. Comput. Phys., 43 (1981), pp. 31–45.

[81] M. EIERMANN AND R. VARGA, *Is the optimal ω best for the SOR iteration method?*, Linear Algebra Appl., 182 (1993), pp. 257–277.

[82] V. EIJKHOUT, *Analysis of parallel incomplete point factorizations*, Linear Algebra Appl., 154–156 (1991), pp. 723–740.

[83] ——, *Beware of unperturbed modified incomplete point factorizations*, in Proceedings of the IMACS International Symposium on Iterative Methods in Linear Algebra, Brussels, Belgium, R. Beauwens and P. de Groen, eds., 1992.

[84] ——, *LAPACK working note 50: Distributed sparse data structures for linear algebra operations*, Tech. Report CS 92-169, Computer Science Department, University of Tennessee, Knoxville, TN, 1992.

[85] ——, *LAPACK working note 51: Qualitative properties of the conjugate gradient and Lanczos methods in a matrix framework*, Tech. Report CS 92-170, Computer Science Department, University of Tennessee, Knoxville, TN, 1992.

[86] V. EIJKHOUT AND B. POLMAN, *Decay rates of inverses of banded M-matrices that are near to Toeplitz matrices*, Linear Algebra Appl., 109 (1988), pp. 247–277.

[87] S. EISENSTAT, *Efficient implementation of a class of preconditioned conjugate gradient methods*, SIAM J. Sci. Statist. Comput., 2 (1981), pp. 1–4.

[88] R. ELKIN, *Convergence theorems for Gauss-Seidel and other minimization algorithms*, Tech. Report 68-59, Computer Science Center, University of Maryland, College Park, MD, Jan. 1968.

[89] H. ELMAN, *Approximate Schur complement preconditioners on serial and parallel computers*, SIAM J. Sci. Statist. Comput., 10 (1989), pp. 581–605.

[90] H. ELMAN AND M. SCHULTZ, *Preconditioning by fast direct methods for non self-adjoint nonseparable elliptic equations*, SIAM J. Numer. Anal., 23 (1986), pp. 44–57.

[91] L. ELSNER, *A note on optimal block-scaling of matrices*, Numer. Math., 44 (1984), pp. 127–128.

[92] V. FABER AND T. MANTEUFFEL, *Necessary and sufficient conditions for the existence of a conjugate gradient method*, SIAM J. Numer. Anal., 21 (1984), pp. 315–339.

[93] G. FAIRWEATHER, A. GOURLAY, AND A. MITCHELL, *Some high accuracy difference schemes with a splitting operator for equations of parabolic and elliptic type*, Numer. Math., 10 (1967), pp. 56–66.

[94] R. FLETCHER, *Conjugate gradient methods for indefinite systems*, in Numerical Analysis Dundee 1975, G. Watson, ed., Berlin, New York, 1976, Springer Verlag, pp. 73–89.

[95] ——, *Conjugate gradient methods for indefinite systems*, vol. 506 of Lecture Notes Math., Springer-Verlag, Berlin, New York, 1976, pp. 73–89.

[96] G. FORSYTHE AND E. STRAUSS, *On best conditioned matrices*, Proc. Amer. Math. Soc., 6 (1955), pp. 340–345.

[97] R. FREUND, *Conjugate gradient-type methods for linear systems with complex symmetric coefficient matrices*, SIAM J. Sci. Statist. Comput., 13 (1992), pp. 425–448.

[98] R. FREUND, G. GOLUB, AND N. NACHTIGAL, *Iterative solution of linear systems*, Tech. Report NA-91-05, Stanford University, Stanford, CA, 1991.

[99] R. FREUND, M. GUTKNECHT, AND N. NACHTIGAL, *An implementation of the look-ahead Lanczos algorithm for non-Hermitian matrices*, SIAM J. Sci. Comput., 14 (1993), pp. 137–158.

[100] R. FREUND AND N. NACHTIGAL, *QMR: A quasi-minimal residual method for non-Hermitian linear systems*, Numer. Math., 60 (1991), pp. 315–339.

[101] ——, *An implementation of the QMR method based on coupled two-term recurrences*, Tech. Report 92.15, RIACS, NASA Ames, Ames, CA, 1992.

[102] R. FREUND AND T. SZETO, *A quasi-minimal residual squared algorithm for non-Hermitian linear systems*, tech. report, RIACS, NASA Ames, Ames, CA, 1991.

[103] R. W. FREUND, *A transpose-free quasi-minimum residual algorithm for non-Hermitian linear systems*, SIAM J. Sci. Comput., 14 (1993), pp. 470–482.

[104] R. W. FREUND, G. H. GOLUB, AND N. M. NACHTIGAL, *Iterative solution of linear systems*, Acta Numerica, (1992), pp. 57–100.

[105] R. W. FREUND, M. H. GUTKNECHT, AND N. M. NACHTIGAL, *An implementation of the look-ahead Lanczos algorithm for non-Hermitian matrices*, SIAM J. Sci. Comput., 14 (1993), pp. 137–158.

[106] R. GLOWINSKI, G. H. GOLUB, G. A. MEURANT, AND J. PÉRIAUX, eds., *Domain Decomposition Methods for Partial Differential Equations*, SIAM, Philadelphia, 1988. Proceedings of the First International Symposium on Domain Decomposition Methods for Partial Differential Equations, Paris, France, January 1987.

[107] G. GOLUB AND D. O'LEARY, *Some history of the conjugate gradient and Lanczos methods*, SIAM Rev., 31 (1989), pp. 50–102.

[108] G. GOLUB AND C. VAN LOAN, *Matrix Computations*, second edition, The Johns Hopkins University Press, Baltimore, 1989.

[109] A. GREENBAUM AND Z. STRAKOS, *Predicting the behavior of finite precision Lanczos and conjugate gradient computations*, SIAM J. Mat. Anal. Appl., 13 (1992), pp. 121–137.

[110] W. D. GROPP AND D. E. KEYES, *Domain decomposition with local mesh refinement*, SIAM J. Sci. Statist. Comput., 13 (1992), pp. 967–993.

[111] I. GUSTAFSSON, *A class of first-order factorization methods*, BIT, 18 (1978), pp. 142–156.

[112] M. H. GUTKNECHT, *A completed theory of the unsymmetric Lanczos process and related algorithms, part II*, Tech. Report 90-16, IPS Research Report, ETH Zürich, Switzerland, 1990.

[113] ——, *The unsymmetric Lanczos algorithms and their relations to Páde approximation, continued fractions and the QD algorithm*, in Proceedings of the Copper Mountain Conference on Iterative Methods, 1990.

[114] ——, *Variants of Bi-CGSTAB for matrices with complex spectrum*, Tech. Report 91-14, IPS ETH, Zürich, Switzerland, 1991.

[115] ——, *A completed theory of the unsymmetric Lanczos process and related algorithms, part I*, SIAM J. Matrix Anal. Appl., 13 (1992), pp. 594–639.

[116] W. HACKBUSCH, *Multi-Grid Methods and Applications*, Springer-Verlag, Berlin, New York, 1985.

[117] ——, *Iterative Lösung großer schwachbestetzter Gleichungssysteme*, Teubner, Stuttgart, 1991.

[118] A. HADJIDIMOS, *On some high accuracy difference schemes for solving elliptic equations*, Numer. Math., 13 (1969), pp. 396–403.

[119] L. HAGEMAN AND D. YOUNG, *Applied Iterative Methods*, Academic Press, New York, 1981.

[120] W. HAGER, *Condition estimators*, SIAM J. Sci. Statist. Comput., 5 (1984), pp. 311–316.

[121] M. HESTENES AND E. STIEFEL, *Methods of conjugate gradients for solving linear systems*, J. Res. Nat. Bur. Stand., 49 (1952), pp. 409–436.

[122] M. R. HESTENES, *Conjugacy and gradients*, in A History of Scientific Computing, Addison-Wesley, Reading, MA, 1990, pp. 167–179.

[123] N. HIGHAM, *Experience with a matrix norm estimator*, SIAM J. Sci. Statist. Comput., 11 (1990), pp. 804–809.

[124] K. JEA AND D. YOUNG, *Generalized conjugate-gradient acceleration of nonsymmetrizable iterative methods*, Linear Algebra Appl., 34 (1980), pp. 159–194.

[125] O. JOHNSON, C. MICCHELLI, AND G. PAUL, *Polynomial preconditioning for conjugate gradient calculations*, SIAM J. Numer. Anal., 20 (1983), pp. 363–376.

[126] ——, *Polynomial preconditioning for conjugate gradient calculation*, SIAM J. Numer. Anal., 20 (1983), pp. 362–376.

[127] M. JONES AND P. PLASSMANN, *Parallel solution of unstructed, sparse systems of linear equations*, in Proceedings of the Sixth SIAM conference on Parallel Processing for Scientific Computing, R. Sincovec, D. Keyes, M. Leuze, L. Petzold, and D. Reed, eds., SIAM, Philadelphia, pp. 471–475.

[128] ——, *A parallel graph coloring heuristic*, SIAM J. Sci. Statist. Comput., 14 (1993), pp. 654–669.

[129] W. JOUBERT, *Lanczos methods for the solution of nonsymmetric systems of linear equations*, SIAM J. Matrix Anal. Appl., 13 (1992), pp. 926–943.

[130] W. KAHAN, *Gauss-Seidel methods of solving large systems of linear equations*, PhD thesis, University of Toronto, 1958.

[131] S. KANIEL, *Estimates for some computational techniques in linear algebra*, Mathematics of Computation, 20 (1966), pp. 369–378.

[132] D. KERSHAW, *The incomplete Cholesky-conjugate gradient method for the iterative solution of systems of linear equations*, J. Comput. Phys., 26 (1978), pp. 43–65.

[133] R. KETTLER, *Analysis and comparison of relaxation schemes in robust multigrid and preconditioned conjugate gradient methods*, in Multigrid Methods, Lecture Notes in Mathematics 960, W. Hackbusch and U. Trottenberg, eds., Springer-Verlag, Berlin, New York, 1982, pp. 502–534.

[134] R. KETTLER, *Linear multigrid methods in numerical reservoir simulation*, PhD thesis, Delft University of Technology, Delft, The Netherlands, 1987.

[135] D. E. KEYES, T. F. CHAN, G. MEURANT, J. S. SCROGGS, AND R. G. VOIGT, eds., *Domain Decomposition Methods For Partial Differential Equations*, SIAM, Philadelphia, 1992. Proceedings of the Fifth International Symposium on Domain Decomposition Methods, Norfolk, VA, 1991.

[136] D. E. KEYES AND W. D. GROPP, *A comparison of domain decomposition techniques for elliptic partial differential equations and their parallel implementation*, SIAM J. Sci. Statist. Comput., 8 (1987), pp. s166 – s202.

[137] S. K. KIM AND A. T. CHRONOPOULOS, *A class of Lanczos-like algorithms implemented on parallel computers*, Parallel Comput., 17 (1991), pp. 763–778.

[138] D. R. KINCAID, J. R. RESPESS, D. M. YOUNG, AND R. G. GRIMES, *IT-PACK 2C: A Fortran package for solving large sparse linear systems by adaptive accelerated iterative methods*, ACM Trans. Math. Soft., 8 (1982), pp. 302–322. Algorithm 586.

[139] C. LANCZOS, *An iteration method for the solution of the eigenvalue problem of linear differential and integral operators*, J. Res. Nat. Bur. Stand., 45 (1950), pp. 255–282.

[140] ———, *Solution of systems of linear equations by minimized iterations*, J. Res. Nat. Bur. Stand., 49 (1952), pp. 33–53.

[141] C. LAWSON, R. HANSON, D. KINCAID, AND F. KROGH, *Basic Linear Algebra Subprograms for FORTRAN usage*, ACM Trans. Math. Soft., 5 (1979), pp. 308–325.

[142] J. MAITRE AND F. MUSY, *The contraction number of a class of two-level methods; an exact evaluation for some finite element subspaces and model problems*, in Multigrid methods, Proceedings, Köln-Porz, 1981, W. Hackbusch and U. Trottenberg, eds., vol. 960 of Lecture Notes in Mathematics, 1982, pp. 535–544.

[143] T. MANTEUFFEL, *The Tchebychev iteration for nonsymmetric linear systems*, Numer. Math., 28 (1977), pp. 307–327.

[144] ———, *An incomplete factorization technique for positive definite linear systems*, Mathematics of Computation, 34 (1980), pp. 473–497.

[145] S. McCORMICK, *Multilevel Adaptive Methods for Partial Differential Equations*, SIAM, Philadelphia, 1989.

[146] S. McCORMICK AND J. THOMAS, *The Fast Adaptive Composite grid (FAC) method for elliptic equations*, Mathematics of Computation, 46 (1986), pp. 439–456.

[147] U. MEIER AND A. SAMEH, *The behavior of conjugate gradient algorithms on a multivector processor with a hierarchical memory*, J. Comput. Appl. Math., 24 (1988), pp. 13–32.

[148] U. MEIER-YANG, *Preconditioned conjugate gradient-like methods for nonsymmetric linear systems*, tech. report, CSRD, University of Illinois, Urbana, IL, April 1992.

[149] J. MEIJERINK AND H. VAN DER VORST, *An iterative solution method for linear systems of which the coefficient matrix is a symmetric M-matrix*, Mathematics of Computation, 31 (1977), pp. 148–162.

[150] ——, *Guidelines for the usage of incomplete decompositions in solving sets of linear equations as they occur in practical problems*, J. Comput. Phys., 44 (1981), pp. 134–155.

[151] R. MELHEM, *Toward efficient implementation of preconditioned conjugate gradient methods on vector supercomputers*, Internat. J. Sumpercomput. Appls., 1 (1987), pp. 77–98.

[152] G. MEURANT, *The block preconditioned conjugate gradient method on vector computers*, BIT, 24 (1984), pp. 623–633.

[153] ——, *Multitasking the conjugate gradient method on the CRAY X-MP/48*, Parallel Comput., 5 (1987), pp. 267–280.

[154] N. NACHTIGAL, S. REDDY, AND L. TREFETHEN, *How fast are nonsymmetric matrix iterations?*, SIAM J. Matrix Anal. Appl., 13 (1992), pp. 778–795.

[155] N. NACHTIGAL, L. REICHEL, AND L. TREFETHEN, *A hybrid GMRES algorithm for nonsymmetric matrix iterations*, Tech. Report 90-7, MIT, Cambridge, MA, 1990.

[156] N. M. NACHTIGAL, *A Look-Ahead Variant of the Lanczos Algorithm and its Application to the Quasi-Minimal Residual Methods for Non-Hermitian Linear Systems*, PhD thesis, MIT, Cambridge, MA, 1991.

[157] Y. NOTAY, *Solving positive (semi)definite linear systems by preconditioned iterative methods*, in Preconditioned Conjugate Gradient Methods, O. Axelsson and L. Kolotilina, eds., vol. 1457 of Lecture Notes in Mathematics, Nijmegen, 1989, pp. 105–125.

[158] ——, *On the robustness of modified incomplete factorization methods*, Internat. J. Comput. Math., 40 (1992), pp. 121–141.

[159] D. O'LEARY, *The block conjugate gradient algorithm and related methods*, Linear Algebra Appl., 29 (1980), pp. 293–322.

[160] ——, *Ordering schemes for parallel processing of certain mesh problems*, SIAM J. Sci. Statist. Comput., 5 (1984), pp. 620–632.

[161] T. C. OPPE, W. D. JOUBERT, AND D. R. KINCAID, *NSPCG user's guide, version 1.0: A package for solving large sparse linear systems by various iterative methods*, Tech. Report CNA–216, Center for Numerical Analysis, University of Texas at Austin, Austin, TX, April 1988.

[162] J. M. ORTEGA, *Introduction to Parallel and Vector Solution of Linear Systems*, Plenum Press, New York and London, 1988.

[163] C. PAIGE, B. PARLETT, AND H. VAN DER VORST, *Approximate solutions and eigenvalue bounds from Krylov subspaces*, Linear Algebra Appl., to appear.

[164] C. PAIGE AND M. SAUNDERS, *Solution of sparse indefinite systems of linear equations*, SIAM J. Numer. Anal., 12 (1975), pp. 617–629.

[165] C. C. PAIGE AND M. A. SAUNDERS, *LSQR: An algorithm for sparse linear equations and sparse least squares*, ACM Trans. Math. Soft., 8 (1982), pp. 43–71.

[166] G. PAOLINI AND G. RADICATI DI BROZOLO, *Data structures to vectorize CG algorithms for general sparsity patterns*, BIT, 29 (1989), pp. 703–718.

[167] B. PARLETT, *The symmetric eigenvalue problem*, Prentice-Hall, London, 1980.

[168] B. N. PARLETT, D. R. TAYLOR, AND Z. A. LIU, *A look-ahead Lanczos algorithm for unsymmetric matrices*, Mathematics of Computation, 44 (1985), pp. 105–124.

[169] D. PEACEMAN AND J. H.H. RACHFORD, *The numerical solution of parabolic and elliptic differential equations*, J. Soc. Indust. Appl. Math., 3 (1955), pp. 28–41.

[170] C. POMMERELL, *Solution of large unsymmetric systems of linear equations*, PhD thesis, Swiss Federal Institute of Technology, Zürich, Switzerland, 1992.

[171] E. POOLE AND J. ORTEGA, *Multicolor ICCG methods for vector computers*, Tech. Report RM 86-06, Department of Applied Mathematics, University of Virginia, Charlottesville, VA, 1986.

[172] A. QUARTERONI, ed., *Domain Decomposition Methods*, Proceedings of the Sixth International Symposium on Domain Decomposition Methods, Como, Italy,, Providence, RI, 1993, AMS. to appear.

[173] G. RADICATI DI BROZOLO AND Y. ROBERT, *Vector and parallel CG-like algorithms for sparse non-symmetric systems*, Tech. Report 681-M, IMAG/TIM3, Grenoble, France, 1987.

[174] J. REID, *On the method of conjugate gradients for the solution of large sparse systems of linear equations*, in Large Sparse Sets of Linear Equations, J. Reid, ed., Academic Press, London, 1971, pp. 231–254.

[175] G. RODRIGUE AND D. WOLITZER, *Preconditioning by incomplete block cyclic reduction*, Mathematics of Computation, 42 (1984), pp. 549–565.

[176] Y. SAAD, *The Lanczos biorthogonalization algorithm and other oblique projection methods for solving large unsymmetric systems*, SIAM J. Numer. Anal., 19 (1982), pp. 485–506.

[177] Y. SAAD, *Practical use of some Krylov subspace methods for solving indefinite and nonsymmetric linear systems*, SIAM J. Sci. Statist. Comput., 5 (1984), pp. 203–228.

[178] ——, *Practical use of polynomial preconditionings for the conjugate gradient method*, SIAM J. Sci. Statist. Comput., 6 (1985), pp. 865–881.

[179] ——, *Krylov subspace methods on supercomputers*, tech. report, RIACS, Moffett Field, CA, September 1988.

[180] ——, *Preconditioning techniques for indefinite and nonsymmetric linear systems*, J. Comput. Appl. Math., 24 (1988), pp. 89–105.

[181] ——, *Krylov subspace methods on supercomputers*, SIAM J. Sci. Statist. Comput., 10 (1989), pp. 1200–1232.

[182] ——, *SPARSKIT: A basic tool kit for sparse matrix computation*, Tech. Report CSRD TR 1029, CSRD, University of Illinois, Urbana, IL, 1990.

[183] ——, *A flexible inner-outer preconditioned GMRES algorithm*, SIAM J. Sci. Comput., 14 (1993), pp. 461–469.

[184] Y. SAAD AND M. SCHULTZ, *Conjugate gradient-like algorithms for solving nonsymmetric linear systems*, Mathematics of Computation, 44 (1985), pp. 417–424.

[185] ——, *GMRES: A generalized minimal residual algorithm for solving nonsymmetric linear systems*, SIAM J. Sci. Statist. Comput., 7 (1986), pp. 856–869.

[186] G. L. G. SLEIJPEN AND D. R. FOKKEMA, *Bi-CGSTAB(ℓ) for linear equations involving unsymmetric matrices with complex spectrum*, Tech. Report 772, University of Utrecht, Deptartment of Mathematics, Utrecht, The Netherlands, 1993.

[187] B. F. SMITH, *Domain decomposition algorithms for partial differential equations of linear elasticity*, Tech. Report 517, Department of Computer Science, Courant Institute, 1990.

[188] P. SONNEVELD, *CGS, a fast Lanczos-type solver for nonsymmetric linear systems*, SIAM J. Sci. Statist. Comput., 10 (1989), pp. 36–52.

[189] R. SOUTHWELL, *Relaxation Methods in Theoretical Physics*, Clarendon Press, Oxford, 1946.

[190] H. STONE, *Iterative solution of implicit approximations of multidimensional partial differetntial equations*, SIAM J. Numer. Anal., 5 (1968), pp. 530–558.

[191] P. SWARZTRAUBER, *The methods of cyclic reduction, Fourier analysis and the FACR algorithm for the discrete solution of Poisson's equation on a rectangle*, SIAM Rev., 19 (1977), pp. 490–501.

[192] C. TONG, *A comparative study of preconditioned Lanczos methods for nonsymmetric linear systems*, Tech. Report SAND91-8240, Sandia Nat. Lab., Livermore, CA, 1992.

[193] A. VAN DER SLUIS, *Condition numbers and equilibration of matrices*, Numer. Math., 14 (1969), pp. 14–23.

[194] A. VAN DER SLUIS AND H. VAN DER VORST, *The rate of convergence of conjugate gradients*, Numer. Math., 48 (1986), pp. 543–560.

[195] H. VAN DER VORST, *Iterative solution methods for certain sparse linear systems with a non-symmetric matrix arising from PDE-problems*, J. Comput. Phys., 44 (1981), pp. 1–19.

[196] ——, *A vectorizable variant of some ICCG methods*, SIAM J. Sci. Statist. Comput., 3 (1982), pp. 350–356.

[197] ——, *Large tridiagonal and block tridiagonal linear systems on vector and parallel computers*, Parallel Comput., 5 (1987), pp. 45–54.

[198] ——, *(M)ICCG for 2D problems on vector computers*, in Supercomputing, A.Lichnewsky and C.Saguez, eds., North-Holland, 1988. Also as Report No.A-17, Data Processing Center, Kyoto University, Kyoto, Japan, December 17, 1986.

[199] ——, *High performance preconditioning*, SIAM J. Sci. Statist. Comput., 10 (1989), pp. 1174–1185.

[200] ——, *ICCG and related methods for 3D problems on vector computers*, Computer Physics Communications, (1989), pp. 223–235. Also as Report No.A-18, Data Processing Center, Kyoto University, Kyoto, Japan, May 30, 1987.

[201] ——, *The convergence behavior of preconditioned CG and CG-S in the presence of rounding errors*, in Preconditioned Conjugate Gradient Methods, O. Axelsson and L. Y. Kolotilina, eds., vol. 1457 of Lecture Notes in Mathematics, Berlin, New York, 1990, Springer-Verlag.

[202] ——, *Bi-CGSTAB: A fast and smoothly converging variant of Bi-CG for the solution of nonsymmetric linear systems*, SIAM J. Sci. Statist. Comput., 13 (1992), pp. 631–644.

[203] H. VAN DER VORST AND J. MELISSEN, *A Petrov-Galerkin type method for solving Ax = b where A is symmetric complex*, IEEE Trans. Magnetics, 26 (1990), pp. 706–708.

[204] H. VAN DER VORST AND C. VUIK, *GMRESR: A family of nested GMRES methods*, Tech. Report 91-80, Delft University of Technology, Faculty of Tech. Math., Delft, The Netherlands, 1991.

[205] J. VAN ROSENDALE, *Minimizing inner product data dependencies in conjugate gradient iteration*, Tech. Report 172178, ICASE, NASA Langley Research Center, 1983.

[206] R. VARGA, *Matrix Iterative Analysis*, Prentice-Hall Inc., Englewood Cliffs, NJ, 1962.

[207] P. VASSILEVSKI, *Preconditioning nonsymmetric and indefinite finite element matrices*, J. Numer. Alg. Appl., 1 (1992), pp. 59–76.

[208] V. VOEVODIN, *The problem of non-self-adjoint generalization of the conjugate gradient method is closed*, U.S.S.R. Comput. Maths. and Math. Phys., 23 (1983), pp. 143–144.

[209] H. F. WALKER, *Implementation of the GMRES method using Householder transformations*, SIAM J. Sci. Statist. Comput., 9 (1988), pp. 152–163.

[210] P. WESSELING, *An Introduction to Multigrid Methods*, Wiley, Chichester, 1991.

[211] O. WIDLUND, *A Lanczos method for a class of non-symmetric systems of linear equations*, SIAM J. Numer. Anal., 15 (1978), pp. 801–812.

[212] D. YOUNG, *Iterative solution of large linear systems*, Academic Press, New York, 1971.

[213] H. YSERENTANT, *On the multilevel splitting of finite element spaces*, Numer. Math., 49 (1986), pp. 379–412.

Index